# FATAL ILLUSION

# FATAL ILLUSION

## DREAMS, DRUGS, DEATH AND REDEMPTION

A BIOGRAPHY ON THE LIFE OF
JUAN PABLO CASTILLO
"CONTRACT KILLER"
FOR THE
"MEDELLÍN COCAINE CARTEL"

LUZ GARCIA

Library of Congress Control Number:                         2012911467
ISBN:                Softcover                         978-1-4633-3225-9
                     Ebook                             978-1-4633-3226-6

GARCIA, LUZ – AUTHOR.
"A FATAL ILLUSION"
Juan Pablo Castillo's journey into darkness, and back into the hands of "God".

NON-FICTION

1 Drug Cartel Assassinations (INTERNATIONAL)
2 COCAINE CARTELS (INTERNATIONAL)
3 ORGANIZED CRIME OF COCAINE TRADE (INTERNATIONAL)
4 Personal Redemption Of Mr. JUAN PABLO CASTILLO.

This book was printed in the United States of America.

**To order additional copies of this book, contact:**
Palibrio
1663 Liberty Drive
Suite 200
Bloomington, IN 47403
Tel: 877.407.5847
Fax: +1.812.355.1576
orders@palibrio.com
408392

# CONTENTS

## PART 1
### "CARTEL"

## PART 2
### "INNOCENCE LOST"

## PART 3
### "AN ANGRY MAN"

# PART 4

## "REDEMPTION"

# PART 5

## "GLADIATOR SCHOOL"

# F O R E W O R D

The following story is true. Some names, dates and places have been changed to protect innocent parties and their families from retribution or retaliation.

All events in this book actually took place, and are taken from my memories of their occurrence.

Any actual conversations and telephone calls have been reconstructed, and the authors have used journalistic license where needed to clarify certain passages.

"Juan Pablo Castillo"

# INTRODUCTION

Like the arms of an octopus, the tentacles of our "Cartel" reach "world-wide", encompassing the globe. Our organization, the "Medellin Cartel", has tens of thousands on its payroll, including police officers, detectives, police chiefs, judges, commissioners, prosecutors, senators, congressmen, governors, heads of state, presidents, Drug Enforcement Agencies, military commanders, border patrol agents, customs agents, Coast Guard Commanders, prison guards, jailers, and an international web of Private Investigators and criminal informants.

We control the transit of our product (COCAINE) by air, land and sea, and often use personal custom-built submarines for underwater shipping when it is necessary to do so, and have done so for years, unknown to the Major Navies of the World.

With millions of customers worldwide that we supply with cocaine, and the hundreds of billions of dollars involved, we have to keep a tight rein on our employees, as sometimes the lure of so much money to be made can cause some of them to become greedy. That can become very unhealthy for them.

My job was to hunt down those people that took what belonged to the "Medellin Cartel", and to make them pay with their lives, and recover our money by whatever means necessary.

My name is "Juan Pablo Castillo", and I worked for Mr. Pedro Diaz for years as their most rusted enforcer and hired assassin.

# INTRODUCTION

# CHAPTER 1

## "You Cannot Hide"
### 1980

A ceiling fan spins slowly in the dining room of an expensive house in a well to do neighborhood in Medellin, Colombia. It's slight breeze making wispy swirls of the smoke coming from the "Lucky Strike" cigarette held by Juan Pablo "El-Loco" Castillo. He is a big man, standing over 6 feet tall, He is powerfully built, with a barrel chest, and his muscles are toned by years of exercise.

In this, his smoking room, he holds in his hand a glass of Chivas Regal #21, a fine and very expensive scotch whiskey, his favorite after dinner drink. He's dinner, sirloin steak with twin lobster tails, and his favorite dessert pecan pie, sit well in his stomach, having been prepared by his personal chef and served to him by his mind, dressed in only an apron and a smile.

The telephone rings beside his easy chair, and he puts out his cigarette as he picks up the gold plated handset and places it next to his right ear.

"Yes", Jessie says into the mouthpiece?

Hey "Loco", says Marcos, Juan Pablo's friend and business associate in the Cartel.

"I just finished dinner, "Marcos", so how are you doing this evening"?

"Fine Juan Pablo; just fine". "Say, listen, call me back on the cell phone, ok.

Juan Pablo breaks the connection momentarily, and punches in Marcos' cell number, which is answered on the first ring.

(MARCOS) — "Juan Pablo, I just got a call from the boss, and they're located "Carlos"?

(JUAN PABLO) – "I knew it was just a matter of time before we found him". "I can't believe he was so stupid as to believe that he could steal almost 2 million dollars worth of coke, about 30 kilos from us, and just disappear". "By the way, where did they find him at?

(MARCOS)– "Talk about stupidity, Juan Pablo, but can you believe it, that "dumb-ass" is right here in "Medellin", not even 30 minutes away from us"?

(JUAN PABLO)- "You're joking, Marcos, no one is that stupid"

(MARCOS)- "I'm not kidding, "El-Loco", he's just a few minutes from here?"

(JUAN PABLO)- "Come on over here, Marcos, I want to see your new Cadillac anyway. We'll discuss our next move when you get here, ok."

(Marcos)- "Be there in a few minutes, Juan Pablo". (CLICK)

Replacing the handset back on its cradle, Juan Pablo shakes his head at how totally idiotic some people can be.

"Carlos", one of our many associates in New York City, had been a trusted and very efficient distributor. He was made a "multi-millionaire" many times over by our drug cartel.

But, as sometimes happens, he got greedy, and decided to keep 30 kilos of cocaine belonging to the Medellin Cartel for himself.

It was just a matter of time before one of our many employees world-wide found him. We have people in our employ from all walks of life that act as our eyes and ears. It is very difficult, if not impossible to hide from us, except for maybe going to another planet, that is.

His thoughts are interrupted by the sounds of his dogs barking loudly, informing him that Marcos has arrived.

He loves those dogs, specially trained Doberman Pincers that are great guard dogs for his expensive home in this nice suburb.

His house, worth $900,000.00 is one of his many houses he keeps in different countries.

He furnishes them expensively and very tastefully, as he likes to be surrounded by nice things, especially beautiful women.

He has lost count of the many hundreds of thousands of dollars that he has spent to entertain, and be entertained by, beautiful young sexy women. His sexual prowess is legendary among women in Medellin, Colombia, and he always has a woman on his arm, or in his bed.

"Come in my friend," Juan Pablo says to Marcos? "Nice car, but did you have to get a black one again"?

"Aw, come on, "Loco"; you know that black is my favorite color"?

"Marcos, how many times do I have to tell you, black is a shade, not a color"?

"Well, whatever, I had it "bullet proofed" in the doors, windows and windshield, and the bottom is also reinforced underneath to help protect against bombs. You can't be too careful these days, especially in this business."

"Nice work, Marcos, but we have some business to take care of now, as the boss wants an example made of Carlos"?

"Do you have any ideas of how we can go about accomplishing this, as we'll need a ruse of some kind to be able to get close to Carlos"? "Do you have anything in mind, Marcos"?

"No problem, Juan Pablo. I have just the kind of thing in mind that never fails, as it is fed by greed & money. Carlos seems to have an over abundance of greed at the moment, and he'll walk right into it, so to speak".

"I have a friend, "Diego," that lives in that neighborhood, Juan Pablo, and he is also a professional photographer, like myself. He knows Carlos, but he doesn't know that we're looking for him. I'll give him a call and see what I can set up, Juan Pablo"?

Marcos pulls out his cellphone and punches some buttons

(Diego)- "Hello," Diego says, as he answers his phone at home.

(Marcos)- "Hey Diego, how you doing old buddy"?

(Diego)- "OH, alright I guess. I just finished processing some photos from a wedding & shot yesterday. They turned out pretty good, as usual."

(Marcos) – "Fine, Fine! Say, how are the wife and kids doing these days? Everything ok with them?"

(Diego)– "They're happy I just sent them off to "Rio" for a short vacation. They'll have fun, I've seen, as she has an old school friend that lives there."

(Marcos) - "Good, good; I'm sure they'll enjoy themselves down there. I've been there several times myself on business, and I can tell you, "Rio" is off the chain!"

"Anyway, I called you for a favor. I have a friend that has twenty-kilos, and I was thinking that you may know of someone who would be interested in doing some business. If you can hook me up with someone, I'll pay you a sizable commission for putting it together for me, Diego.

(Diego)– "Well, as a matter of fact, I do have someone in mind that I believe would be interested in doing some business with you. Let me make a call to him, and I'll call you back when I get a hold of him and find out if he wants to some business, ok."

(Marcos)- "Sounds good, Diego. Let me know as soon as you can, as my friend is anxious to do a deal. Take care now, my friend." (CLICK)

Marcos turns to Juan Pablo in the living room.

"Juan Pablo, my friend Diego is going to call Carlos and set up a meet for us, as he says Carlos will probably want to do a deal."

"He says he'll call me back after he talks to him."

"Excellent", says Juan Pablo! "But you do realize that after killing Carlos, that we can't leave any witnesses, and Diego we'll know of our meeting with Carlos, and could tie us to his murder".

"I understand that, Juan Pablo", says Marcos. "I wish it didn't have to be that way, but in this business, you can't afford to have any loose ends." "I'll make sure that the commission I mentioned to Diego goes to his wife and kids, kind of a gift from me to her in her time of sorrow, shall I say.

"That sounds good," says Juan Pablo. "That's why I like working with you, Marcos, you can think quickly on your feet."

"Stay here tonight, and have a few drinks to relax", says Juan Pablo, as he walks out through his sliding glass doors toward the swimming pool.

"Sounds good to me, Juan Pablo", replies Marcos, walking over to the bar on the patio, facing the pool.

"Would you like me to make you a drink"? "As I remember, it is usually Chivas Regal #21 straight up, double, correct?"

"You have an excellent memory, Marcos"!

"Here you go", Juan Pablo, "Chivas on the rocks"! "I'm finishing off your bottle of "Tequila"", I'm afraid".

"Go ahead," says Juan Pablo, "I've got 5 more bottles under the bar." "I just re-stocked the bar yesterday"

Juan Pablo walks toward the pool, sipping his drink and contemplating the job he has to do for the "boss" of the cartel. Although he works with Marcos on the cartel's business dealings, he has never trusted him in any way.

Every time he looks at him, he thinks he's standing in front of the American actor, "Clint Eastwood". He can't get over how much "Marcos" looks like him, all the way down to the way he always dresses, with his sombrero and Mexican poncho and western cowboy boots.

He knows that "Marcos" is a professional photographer and can pretty much arrange anything for the cartel, but what gets under his skin the most is how easily "Marcos" will kill someone without a second thought.

He has heard stories from the others in their organization about how "cold-blooded" Marcos is, and how much of a back-stabber he is.

"Marcos" is a very rich man, and many say that he got that way in the cartel from many of the murders he has done for the boss.

"Dangerous" doesn't even begin to describe him.

Juan Pablo's thoughts are interrupted by Marcos' constant facing back and forth in front of the outside patio bar.

He can tell Marcos is getting himself all worked up over something, as Marcos is getting more and more tense and agitated every minute.

He looks at Marcos over the rim of his cocktail glass as he drinks from it, and sees that the veins are permanent, and sticking out on his neck and forehead.

"What the hell's bothering you"? asks Juan Pablo, as he walks over to the patio bar and finishes off his drink, refilling the glass with scotch.

Marcos turns to look at him and slams his drink down on the bar, shattering the glass and cutting his hand, which he doesn't even notice.

"It's just that I can't get over how Carlos stated thirty kilos from us, and thought he could get away with it so easy"!

"We've been doing business with him for years now, "El-Loco", and he's always been dependable and taken care of business."

"I kind of liked the guy when I first met him, just before he went back to New York City with his first shipment. He set me up with that little Swedish blond girl, "Arla", the one that looked kind of like "Heather Locklear" in the bikini. She screwed me every which way but loose, Juan Pablo", "I'll never forget it"! "And now, "El-Loco", we've got to kill the dumb-ass"!

"It's out of our hands now", says Juan Pablo, as he hands Marcos a clean hand cloth to staunch the flow of blood from his cut hand.

Marcos takes the cloth for a moment, then tosses it aside, bringing his hand up to his mouth. He tastes the blood on his lips as he sucks on the cut fingers, feeling the warm liquid flow over his tongue as it begins to fill his mouth. His eyes turn jet-black as he grins and swallows.

Juan Pablo just stares at him for a moment, not knowing what to say or think.

"Has Marcos gone insane"? Juan Pablo thinks to himself, as he tosses back his glass and finishes his scotch in one large swallow.

"Yes, I will kill the little bastard," says Marcos, seemingly coming out from under some kind of self-induced trance, "and I'll enjoy every second of it too, "El-Loco"!"

Juan Pablo, looking at Marcos intently, seeing his dark eyes and the deadly intent behind them, does not doubt that for a single moment.

# CHAPTER 2

......................................................

# Not Long To Live

The morning sun rises silently as the birds begin to chirp, and tiny green lizards scamper quickly among the tall grass, chasing their prey of flies and insects. Crickets are heard chirping in the distance.

Juan Pablo, awake before dawn as usual, sits on the patio at his table under the sun umbrella. He is attired in a crisp white shirt and pants, tailored to fit perfectly, and his favorite hand-made itallion shoes without socks. He's early morning raising a habit he picked up in the Colombian army.

Across from him, Marcos, still half asleep, is eating a breakfast of large spicy link sausages along with homemade English muffins, crispy hash-brown, and some strong Colombian coffee.

"Your cook did a wonderful job for my breakfast, Juan Pablo"!

"She should", says El-Loco. "I pay her enough"!

"Kind of getting some on the side too, eh"?

Juan Pablo starts to reply but is cut short by the chirping ring-tone of Marcos' cell phone.

Marcos picks his phone up off the table and punches a button, placing it next to his right ear as he chews on the thick sausage.

"Yeah",? says Marcos into the phone.

"Hey Marcos", Diego says, "I called my friend last night, and he says he definitely wants to do some business with you. He's sitting with me here at the house right now. Do you want us to meet you somewhere?"

"No, no, that won't be necessary, Diego," says Marcos.

"We're only about 20 minutes away, so my friend and I will pick you two up, and we'll discuss our transaction together."

"I'll be using my jeep, Diego"; says Marcos.

"Sounds good to me," says Diego, giving his friend Carlos the thumbs-up sign with his right hand.

Carlos breaks into a broad smile as Diego hangs up his phone.

"They'll be here in 20 minutes", says Diego to his guest.

"Great", says Carlos, as he lights a Havana cigar with his gold-plated cigarette lighter.

Just as they're finishing their drinks, they hear the whining sound of a jeeps' engine coming down the street.

"That must be them now", Carlos says to Diego, as they put down their drinks and step outside into the early morning sunlight.

"Hey Diego", says Marcos, as he and Juan Pablo pull into the driveway in the jeep.

"We'll go in the jeep", says Marcos. "My friend is waiting in another neighborhood for us, to discuss the deal".

"That ok with you, Carlos"? says Diego to his friend.

"No problem at all, Diego"! Let's get this done and over with.

Both Carlos & Diego get into the back seats of the jeep as Juan Pablo holds back the passenger front seat for them.

Marcos takes the wheel and begins driving, glancing behind him through the rear-view mirror for a moment at the two men.

Juan Pablo pulls out his first allotted cigarette of the day, a "Lucky Strike", and searches his pockets for his lighter.

Unable to find it, he suddenly remembers that he left it on his patio table by the pool.

"Marcos, let me see your lighter for a moment I left mine back at the house".

"Sure, Juan Pablo", says Marcos, as he passes his gold Zippo to him, noticing that Juan Pablo has his gold-plated .45 caliber automatic in a shoulder holster, which is peeking out from under his jacket.

Juan Pablo, passing it back to him after lighting his "Lucky", silently nods his head to Marcos as he sees that he has his Ingram .45 caliber machine pistol tucked down under his belt.

After several minutes of driving, they approach a very isolated, yet very expensive neighborhood that they knew, and pointed out the house where their friend was waiting for them, to discuss their deal.

"That's the house right over there", Marcos says to Diego and Carlos.

"We'll park up the road a little bit, as my friend said he doesn't want any cars parked in front of the house".

They pulled up about 100 yards from the house and turned off the ignition.

Marcos gets out of the driver's side and walks toward the front of the jeep.

Juan Pablo opens his passenger side door and steps out, holding the passenger seat forward as first Diego, then Carlos climb out of the vehicle.

As Juan Pablo closes the door, he begins walking about five feet behind Diego and Carlos, who are oblivious to the danger.

Without any warning, Juan Pablo hears the muffled sounds of bullets being fired in rapid succession from behind him, off of his right shoulder.

PFFFFT-PFFFFT-PFFFFT-PFFFFT-PFFFFF"!

He feels flocks of warm, wet liquid splatter onto his face, staining his sunglasses, and is momentarily stunned as he realizes that Marcos has already pulled out his Ingram .45 caliber machine-pistol with a 6 inch silencer attached, and is spraying both Carlos and Diego with a full clip.

Juan Pablo freezes as he sees the large caliber bullets tear into the two men, and bloody holes appear in their backs in front of him.

Carlos, with a surprised look on his face, spins around several times, and is dead before he hits the ground, his head exploding from one of the slugs that hits him in the left eye.

Diego, though tries to run, and gets about 20 feet from Juan Pablo before he falls to the ground, blood trickling out of his open mouth.

Looking at Juan Pablo, he chokes out the words; "Please, Please, for Gods' sake don't kill me"! "I won't say anything to anyone, I promise I won't; please don't kill me, Juan Pablo"!

Juan Pablo reaches into his jacket to his shoulder holster, and pulls out his .45 caliber automatic, chambering a round.

He kneels down next to Diego.

"Diego, please understand, this is nothing personal, it is just business.

Juan Pablo then places the barrel of the .45 onto under Diego's chin, points it upward, and pulls the trigger, blowing the top off of Diego's' head.

Diego jerks once, then lays still.

Juan Pablo, at that moment in time, doesn't even know who, or what he is, or has become. He stores at Diego's' body, shaking his head from side to side slowly.

His thoughts are interrupted at that moment by a loud, blood curdling scream!

He looks up and sees that a man who had been washing his car had seen the whole incident go down, and was utterly terrified as he ran screaming back into his house.

Juan Pablo, sickened by the killings, holsters his .45 automatic.

Marcos, who had also seen the man, replaced the empty clip in his machine-pistol with a full one, and began walking towards the screaming mans house.

Juan Pablo, seeing this, says to Marcos;

"No, No"! "Vámonos de aquí"!

("No, No"! "Let's get out of here"!

"El quiere vivir mas porque quiere hablar con la policía!"

"(He wants to live more than he wants to talk to the police"!)

Marcos stops momentarily, turns and looks at Juan Pablo, a surprised look in his eyes.

Juan Pablo reaches out and grabs hold of his arm, looks him straight in the eye, and shakes his head from side to side.

"Let's go"! Juan Pablo says, as he begins to walk back toward the jeep.

Marcos reluctantly slips his Ingram .45 back into his belt and joins Juan Pablo at the jeep.

As Marcos gets into the jeep and starts the engine, he look sideways at "El-Loco", wondering why he stopped him from eliminating a witness to the murders.

"Hey "Loco"! What's gotten into you"?

"That man can identify both of us"!

"Marcos", says Juan Pablo, "He knows that we know exactly where he lives"!

"He's not about to jeopardize his life, or the life of any of his family members by sticking his nose in our business." "If the authorities question him, he'll say he heard nothing, and that a swarm of wasps startled him, and chased him into the house this morning".

Taking a cigarette out of his pocket, Marcos lights it and blows smoke towards the windshield, looking back through the rear-view mirror.

"Well, I guess one of us has to use some sense once in awhile", he says to Juan Pablo.

"Do you want me to drop you off at your house, El-Loco?" says Marcos.

"Si"! - Marcos.

After being dropped off by Marcos, Juan Pablo walks out to his patio bar and pours himself a stiff drink, downing it in one gulp as he feels it sting his hot, dry throat.

It is then that it downs on Juan Pablo just how much blood he has on him.

Both his white pants and shirt are covered in dried blood, and his hand-made Itallion shoes are bloody and ruined.

He goes to his walk-in closet and finds a clean set of clothes, takes off the bloody ones, and enjoys a long, hot shower.

Toweling off, he hears his "maid-cook-lover, "Juanita", working in the kitchen, fixing his lunch.

That's one of the many things he likes about her, she is efficient, and she minds her own business, asking no questions of him. That is the main reason he hired her, on top of her being an excellent cook and a warm lover in the night.

He again looks at the bloody clothes before disposing of them

"My God", he says to himself.

"What have I become"?

# CHAPTER 3

·····································

# Cold Blooded Killer

"Such a nice color for a man's' car", thought Marcos, as he pulled into his driveway and shut off the engine of his new Cadillac.

To Marcos, black suited him just fine, as it reflected his moods, personality, and lack of conscience.

Taking his Ingram .45 caliber machine-pistol from the seat next to him, he puts it back under his belt and opens the door, exits the car, and heads for his front door.

Once inside, he locks the door, throwing two dead-bolts he has had installed, securing the house. He then activates his house alarm, pushing several buttons on the activation pad.

He sits down on his custom leather sofa and lights another cigarette, tossing his gold plated Zippo onto the coffee table as he exhales the smoke out of his nostrils slowly.

He likes the style and layout of this 5 bedroom 6 bath house, with its swimming pool and six car garage, as he can keep several of his expensive "toys" in it, and drive them when the mood hits him.

It is one of many houses he has in Colombia, and other cities throughout the world, where he stays while conducting business for the cartel.

This house, in an expensive neighborhood of Medellin, is just the right size for his needs, as it is roomy enough for guests, and, with its steel gate and high-walled fences, is private enough to keep prying and curious eyes away from his activities.

Walking to the bar in the corner of the living room, he takes out a glass and pours himself a double-shot of Tequila, downs it in one gulp, and refills the glass before settling back down on the sofa, bringing his feet up onto the edge of the coffee table and crossing his shiny snake-skin cowboy boots one over the other.

He stares for a moment at the silver tips on the front of the boots, and the intricate and colorful design of the matching snake-skins that were used to make them, and remembers his trip to Dallas, Texas, where he had had them custom-made for him while there.

"The "boss" had contacted him while he was in Los Angeles, and he was instructed to go to Dallas to make sure that an associate named Anibal* had no problems collecting $250,000.00 from a dealer, whom had repeatedly stalled on paying for his lost shipment of cocaine from the cartel.

Arriving at Dallas/Ft. Worth Airport aboard the United Airlines 747, he disembarked from the First Class section into the terminal, going straight to the "Hertz" Rent-a-Car station.

Insisting on a dark sedan, he was pleasantly surprised to be issued a Cadillac "Sedan-De-Ville". Before leaving the airport, after claiming his baggage, he called Anibal and arranged for him to meet him in "Benbrook," a suburb of Ft. Worth, where he had several contacts for weapons he might have a need for if the dealer proved to be stubborn.

Sitting at the booth in McDonalds, he took a large bite out of his second "Big-Mac" and sipped on his large Coke that he had spiked with some Tequila from his glove box in the Cadillac.

As he was finishing up his second sandwich, he noticed a tall, thick-limbed black man with large eyebrows and a double-chin enter the fast-food restaurant through the front doors. He had been told Anibal's general description, and had been told by Anibal what to say to be sure it was him he approached at the McDonalds.

"Hot day today"! stated Marcos, getting up from his booth and walking toward the man.

"Yes, it is hot out there, and I sure could use some help with some air-conditioning, as I'm having problems with it," replied the man, confirming to Marcos that it was indeed Anibal.

"Let's go take a look at your problem", says Marcos, as they both head for the front door.

Once outside, Anibal tells Marcos to follow him in his rental car, as he leads the way to his "ranch-style" house on the edge of the city limits of Dallas.

Once there, they enter the house and Anibal makes them both drinks, which they take outside as they walk towards the stables.

"Nice horses", says Marcos, as he reaches out to stroke the mane of an "appaloosa", with its brown, black and white spotting.

"Yes, he's one of my favorites", says Anibal. "My daughter learned to ride on him, as he's as gentle as a lamb." "His name is "Scout".

"I have several 5 dozen horses, Anibal", replies Marcos, as he looks around the stables, seeing about half a dozen quarter-horses in their stalls

"Mine are purebred "Arabians", says Marcos. "They cost me $750,000.00 a piece, which is quite reasonable considering their bloodline". Saudi Kings and Princes own them and race them frequently there in "Saudi Arabia".

"I can't quite afford that kind of a horse yet," says Anibal, especially right now, as I'm having quite a bit of trouble collecting your money from one of my dealers here".

"Can you contact him on your cell phone"? asks Marcos, "so that I can speak to him"?

"Here's his number", states Anibal, as he writes it down on a slip of paper.

Marcos takes out his own cell phone and punches in the numbers, and hears it ring on the dealers cell phone several times before it is answered by a male voice.

"Yeah, what's up"? says the voice loudly.

"To whom am I speaking to? asks Marcos.

"I'm the man with the plan and a golden ton, got what you want in my gold-plated can", says Tito the dealer.

"What I want is my $250,000.00 owed for several months now, and you have exactly 24 hours to come up with it, Tito, or I will be paying "you" a visit, is that understood"? says Marcos coldly into the cell-phone!

"What the hell"? states Tito!

"You heard me", says Marcos, taking a cigarette out and lighting it before continuing.

"Who the hell is this"? asks Tito!

"Never mind who I am, just have my money ready within 24 hours, and you can stay healthy", replies Marcos.

"Man, I told Ruben I'll pay when I'm damn good and ready, and I ain't ready, you dig where I'm coming from"! says Tito in reply.

"You have 24 hours to get it for me", says Marcos. "I'll call and tell you where to meet me with the money at that time".

"Go to Hell", says Tito, hanging up the phone.

"If he doesn't have the money in 24 hours, I'll make an example of him", states Marcos to Anibal.

Marcos then gets into the rental car and drives into downtown Dallas, noticing on a bank's electronic sign that the temperature outside the car is 104°F.

He then notices a sign advertising custom "hand-made" western boots, and parks the Caddy in front of the shop.

After picking out the snake-skin leather, and having a mold made of his feet, he pays the craftsman $2,196.12 for them, giving his address in Medellin for their delivery in 6 weeks or so.

He spends time at several "Honky-Tonks" in the Dallas area that night, quizzing Anibal on Tito's address, his description, the car he drives, etc.., in preparation for the next day's meeting. He sleeps well that night, accompanied by an 18 year old blond, who charges him $500.00 for the night.

Placing another call to Tito, Marcos, chews on a piece of rare steak as the cell phone rings on Tito's end, at the end of 24 hours.

"Yeah", says Tito into his phone!

"Do you have my money ready"? asks Marcos.

"I told you mister whoever the hell you are I'll pay Ruben when I'm down good and ready"! yells Tito into the phone, before it breaks the call's connection.

Getting into his rental car, Marcos calls his associates in "Benbrook", and tells them he'll be there in an hour.

Arriving in the thriving suburb of Dallas, he sees that "Benbrook" hasn't changed much in the last few years, except for maybe another "fast-food" joint or two.

He pulls into a driveway and kills the engine, getting out of the car into the afternoon dry, Texas heat.

His associate, "Max" steps out of his house and greets him on the front porch, reaching out his hand to shake Marcos'.

"What brings you to these parts"? says Max, as they walk into the modest "split-level" house, feeling the chilled air of the powerful air conditioner hit them pleasantly in the face.

"We're having trouble collecting payment for a shipment that our distributor, "Anibal", fronted to a dealer named Tito", says Marcos, lighting another cigarette with his lighter.

"I called him yesterday from Anibal's ranch, told him he had 24 hours to get my money, but when I called back awhile ago, he tells me to go to hell for the second time. I'm going to make an example of him, and send him and anyone else who gets in the way straight to hell myself," states Marcos. "If he doesn't pay me, he'll get to hell before I do"!

"What will you be needing for the job", asks Max, as he gets up from his easy chair and walks toward the back of the house, stopping in front of a walk in closet.

"Well, I could use an AK-47 with 3 or 4 full clips, and a 9 mm with a silencer".

"No problem", says Max, as he pulls on a string hanging in a corner, and the wall in the back of the closet opens up to reveal a hidden room, filled with weapons of all kinds and many different kinds of grenades.

"This will do just fine", says Marcos, as he grabs an AK-47 with a folding stock out of the display case, along with 4 full clips.

Looking over the automatic pistols, he selects a 9 mm German Luger with an attached silencer, and 3 full clips of ammo.

"This will also work very nicely", says Marcos, as he checks the clips for both the AK-47 and the Luger.

"Need any help, my friend",? asks Max, as they step out of the hidden room and close the wall panel, exiting the closet.

"No, Max", states Marcos. "This won't take long, and I can handle it myself quite easily".

"Ok, but let me know if there's anything else that you need while you're here in Dallas", says Max, as they wrap the weapons in an old wind-breaker to carry out to the car.

"I'll let you know how it goes, Max, and thanks, my friend," states Marcos, as he opens the car door and sits behind the wheel, starting the engine and closing the car door.

He then takes out the piece of paper that Anibal gave him that morning, containing the address of this "idiot," Tito.

Driving through Dallas to that neighborhood, he remembers that the "Southfork" ranch is just about 15 miles west of there. "Nice area", he says to himself as he checks the speedometer, making sure to stay under the speed limit. He doesn't want to get pulled over by the police with a machine gun and silenced 9 mm onto.

Waiting until the sun is setting that evening, Marcos packs about ¼ mile from the address, concealing the car behind some trees off the road.

He takes the weapons out of the car, and after checking them, places the Luger under his belt, while slinging the AK-47 over his left shoulder.

After placing the clips in his pockets, he walks toward the large two story house, which is surrounded by a stone wall, and ornamental gate. As he gets close to the front gate, he sees a big German Shepherd dog running toward the entrance.

Having brought some beef jerky with him as a snack, it now came in handy, as he would need to silence the guard dog, or it would spoil the element of surprise he needed at the moment.

Taking out the jerky and tearing open the wrapper, he threw it over the fence toward the dog, while softly saying "here boy, here boy" several times.

As the dog ate the jerky and looked at him, he pulled out the 9 mm Luger and fired one shot into the dogs head, dropping him instantly in his tracks.

He hated to have to do that as he loved German Shepherds, and had several of them at the ranch back in Medellin.

Then, climbing over the stone wall, he silently walked toward the house, the 9 mm automatic in his right hand.

Staying behind some trees in the yard for cover, he looked at the front room windows, about 50 ft. away, and saw a large black male walking by the window.

Waiting a few minutes to make sure he was alone, he walked up to the house, and with his right foot, kicked in the front door.

As the door broke down in splintering pieces of wood, he stepped inside the house, aiming the Luger toward the living room where he knew Tito was standing.

As Tito reacted to his door bursting open, he reached toward the .357 magnum sitting on his coffee table.

"I wouldn't do that if I were you, that is, if you want to live", said Marcos, as he stepped toward Tito, pointing the 9 mm at his head.

"You had 24 hours to get my money for me; and your time is up"!

"Ah, ok man", I'll get it for you, just don't kill me, ok man", screams Tito, as he backs up with his hands over his head.

"Where is it",? asks Marcos, as he cocks the Luger and points it back at Tito, who is shaking very badly, and scared to death that he's about to die.

"It's in the safe, ok, behind the painting above the fireplace"!

"Open it now", states Marcos.

Tito walks over to the picture and removes it from the wall, revealing a wall safe.

He turns it several times and pulls it open, taking out stocks of 50 and 100 dollar bills.

He counts out $250,000.00 and places it on the coffee table, shaking so violently that he drops stocks of bills several times and has to stop to pick them up again.

"No, Tito", says Marcos, "all of it"!

"What the hell do you mean all of it,"? asks Tito. "I only owe you $250,000.00 dollars"!

"You've been playing games with Anibal, and are two months late in paying, Tito", says Marcos

"You owe me interest for two months, plus spoiling my vacation in Los Angeles yesterday"!

"I should kill you where you stand, and I just might if you piss me off anymore", but for now, put all of the money from the safe on the table, and sit down on the floor, looking at the wall", says Marcos, beginning to get bored with Tito.

After Tito places all of the money from the safe on the table, he gets down on the floor, facing the wall.

Marcos then walks up behind him and places the Luger's barrel in Tito's left ear, and cocks it with the top slide!

Shaking so hard he can barely speak, Tito says; "Don't kill me, man! Please don't kill me"! "OH God"!

Marcos says to him, "goodbye Tito", and squeezes the trigger.

"AHRRRRHH"! screams Tito, as he hears the loudest "click" he's ever heard in his life! He's breathing becomes erratic, and he nearly faints.

Marcos then looks down at the puddle of urine expanding around Tito's pants, and realizes he's scared the piss out of him, which was his intention, as while Tito was emptying the safe, he had slipped the clip out of the Luger and placed it in his shirt pocket.

Then, when he placed the barrel of the 9 mm in Tito's ear and cocked it, he'd palmed the bullet that had been in the chamber, and slipped it into his other hand, leaving the gun empty.

Now, inserting the clip back into the Luger, Marcos chambers a bullet and places it back in Tito's ear.

"Tito, if I ever hear of you causing us anymore trouble, of any kind whatsoever, I will personally come hunt you down and blow your stupid brains out of your head. Do you understand me?"

"Yeah man, I got you loud and clear, no more problems, ok man"!

"Good boy", says Marcos, as he lays the hammer down on the Luger gently and places it under his belt.

"Where's your new car"? asks Marcos, motioning Tito to get up off the floor.

"It's in the garage", states Tito. "Why do you want to see my car?"

"I was told you purchased a new Rolls Royce". "I love nice cars, Tito"! "I have two Rolls Royces myself".

They start walking out of the house and towards the 2 car garage through the darkening night, hearing the frogs croak in unison among the tall grass.

Opening the garage door, Marcos sees two very expensive automobiles sitting in the building.

One is an 82 Bentley, and the other is a brand new chocolate brown Rolls Royce Corniche convertible.

"Nice cars", he says, as he pulls the AK-47 around off of his left shoulder and begins firing first at the Bentley with one clip, then unloads a second full clip into the Corniche convertible, riddling the cars with bullet holes and exploding glass as the deafening sounds of the muzzle blasts fills the night air.

Tito, watching from twenty feet away, only stares helplessly as his pride & joys are destroyed by a fusilade of bullets that he realized could have been used to cut him in half.

"No more problems, Tito", says Marcos, as he backs toward the front gate and disappears into the night.

"Did you kill him"? asks Anibal, as Marcos walks in his front door.

"No, Ruben"; says Marcos, as he sits down and lights a cigarette. "There is no need for that".

"I was told in Los Angeles to make sure there were no problems in collecting our money from him. I was not instructed to kill him"!

"I do not think he'll be late with anymore payments, or cause you anymore problems in the future".

"Thanks Marcos", says Anibal, as Marcos gets up and leaves the house, heading for the car. "Drive safely, my friend"!

His custom snake-skin cowboy boots arrived about 5 weeks later by air-express delivery. They fit his feet perfectly, and he loved the quality of the workmanship, and the intricate design of the snake-skin leather. He called and ordered 10 more pairs in various exotic leathers and colors.

Removing his feet from the coffee table, he picked up his Ingram .45 caliber and removed the empty clip. Clearing the chamber, he studied the weapon for a few moments, admiring the workmanship.

"Good design", he says to himself, as he unscrews the 6 inch long custom-made silencer and places it on the coffee table in front of him.

It is only one of many of the weapons he has in his large collection of firearms and submachine guns. He also has over a dozen crossbows of different makes.

Reaching under his couch, he pulls out his gun cleaning kit and begins to wipe down the Ingram.

He then places an oily cloth strip in the barrel rod, and runs it through the barrel to clean out the remnants of the day's work on Carlos and Diego.

"How many does that make"? he thinks to himself, as he places the Ingram under his couch pillow, in case he needs to get to it quickly. You never know in this business.

Is it 220, or 225? He doesn't really know, as he pretty much lost count at around 200 kills.

Marcos loves his job working for the cartel. He makes a ridiculous amount of money taking care of business for the cartel's boss, and the amounts that they pay him has made him a very, very wealthy man, on top of what he makes smuggling cocaine for them. Between contract killings and smuggling cocaine, he has made close to a Billion dollars. Most people cannot comprehend how much money cocaine generates.

Yes, life is good, if you are good at what you do, he thought to himself, and he was considered one of the best at what he did for the cartel.

Killing people came easily for Marcos, as he feels nothing whenever he pulls the trigger, ending someone's life.

He can barely remember ever feeling any emotions in his life, except anger and hate and a lot of bitterness towards people.

Hatred now warms his blood.

Even as a child he hardly ever felt loved by his parents, as his mother and father were divorced around the time he was born.

His earliest memories are of being spanked and then beaten by his mother until his arms and legs were bleeding.

His mother never even said "I Love You" to him, which tore his heart out as a child, and made him cold and bitter.

He did love his dad, but hardly ever saw him while he was growing up into a man. Although he loved his father, he had absolutely no respect for him at all.

His mother was never home with him, and he resented that very much.

He had battled up his anger, and now, whenever he did a job, or "contrast," he could easily pull the trigger, thinking of the people he hated as he imagined he was killing them over and over and over again. It made him feel better.

It got to where it put a smile on his face each time he saw the bloody bullet holes appear on the bodies of those that he murdered, and he got a big kick out of them doing their "death-dance" as the bullets tore into their soft flesh and bones, releasing a flow of warm red blood.

The men, women and children that he killed, it never mattered to him at all, as when it is your time to go, you go, and if your caught in the wrong place at the wrong time, it was not his problem.

He has never been caught for murder, as he has never left a living witness to any of the killings he has done. That is why people call him "The Ice Man". He is very deadly and ruthless.

If you're dead, you can't testify against someone, can you.

At 6' 2" tall and weighing 250 lbs, he was a big man, with brown eyes and curly brown hair with a burgundy & reddish hue in it.

He looked as ruggedly handsome as the American actor, Clint Eastwood, and even dressed like him with his poncho, sombrero and cowboy boots.

That was his favorite style of clothing.

OH, he wore regular clothes as well, but many times you could spot him in clubs and discos in the latest style of tuxedos.

He owned almost 100 suits of every color, and almost as many tuxedos.

His dozens of pairs of shoes, all of them custom-made, cost 6 to 7 hundred dollars a pair.

Life had been good to him after joining the Medellin Cartel, and he hasn't looked back since. He is their highest paid killer and cocaine smuggler, as no one is better at either than he is.

He was very well connected in the cartel, and was filthy rich because of it.

Of the over 800 million dollars he has made in the years of working for the cartel, he has had to spread it around in over 100 banks and safe deposit boxes around the world, after laundering it through legitimate businesses to keep the huge amount of his criminal monetary fortune from arousing the banking and federal authorities suspicions.

His pocket money is always 10-20 thousand in 100 dollar bills, as he will carry nothing smaller than that. His change is usually gold AFRICAN KRUGERANDS and he carries 20 to 30 of them in his pockets for luck. It has worked for him for years, so why stop.

He didn't believe in smuggling cocaine at 20 or 30 kilos at a time, like other drug smugglers did.

No, that doesn't work for him, not at all!

Marcos smuggled cocaine for the Medellin cartel by the "ton", almost 1000 kilos at a time, and he made the cartel very happy with him, as usual.

He never let anything or anyone stop him from doing so successfully, because if he couldn't pay people to look the other way for a good amount of money, then he'd kill their friends and family members until they did his bidding. One way or another, he got his way.

He was much admired by many in the criminal underworld for his courage and ruthlessness, and for his determination to get his shipments through successfully.

That was one of the reasons that many low enforcement agencies had dubbed him a member of a new breed of criminal.

He was, by their description, a "Super-Criminal"!

• • • • • • • • •

He thought about that or a moment as he poured himself another shot of Tequila into his glass.

"Ha-Ha", he chuckled, "a Super-Criminal"!

"Can you beat that"! "What were the "Federales" going to come up with next"?

OH, they tried to stop him, of course, but they were too stupid and too slow in trying to do so.

He'd let them think they were successful in fighting their "silly war on drugs" against the cartel by having an "associate", who the police thought was an "insider", tell them about a shipment, and it's route and time of transport.

He'd literally give them 30-40 kilos of cocaine so that they'd think they'd made a big bust.

They were so dumb that they didn't realize that their "bust" was orchestrated by him on purpose, to make them concentrate their agency's manpower in catching the "cigarette boat" that was speeding toward the Florida coast with the small 30-40 kilo shipment.

They didn't realize that while they were going after the "cigarette" boat with the 30-40 kilos, that a private, large sailboat or personal submarine was bringing 2000 to 4000 pounds or more to their coast by another route!

That is one of the many things that he loved about the authorities. Most of them could be bought off. He knows that most people are greedy when it comes to money, and he uses this to his advantage in the drug business of the Medellin Cartel.

He knew that every man has his price, and that, if the money is right, the authorities couldn't really care less what he was transporting, as long as they got a cut of the money, and there was always lots of money to go around.

When shipping cocaine by the "tons", it was nothing for him to pay out three or four million dollars to make sure that the shipment got through to its destination.

If someone got too greedy or balked at accepting a payoff, or wanted to play "hero cop", he had their family members raped and killed, one by one, in front of them, before cutting off their sex organs, stuffing it into their mouth, then killing them.

Sometimes he'd cut out their heart. At other times he'd machine gun them. And other times hed cut their heads off. Whatever the mood of the moment usually dictated his method of execution. He used his admittedly sick imagination to come up with different ways to kill them.

Once, after being "double-crossed," he tied up a judge and his wife and children. Then he killed the son immediately in front of him, had 8 of his men rape his wife and eleven year old daughter repeatedly in his presents, then cut them both open to disembowel them, letting them painfully die agonizing deaths in front of the Judge, before blowing his head off with a shotgun.

This was done to send a message to others that it is very dangerous and suicidal to cross him.

At times when an associate gets greedy, he is called upon to "weed the garden" so to speak.

Diego, whom he had known for years, had to be eliminated as a witness as he never left any witnesses alive to possibly testify against him for a killing.

He'd been a good "friend" for many years, and they'd had many good times together, fishing, hunting and boating. They'd had many laughs together about life's adventures. He'd used him to get close to Carlos, then had to kill the both of them together.

But, what is a "friend"? He had none. He had no one that he held in that high regard, and never, ever trusted anyone completely.

He was always looking over his shoulder, not just for the policia or "federales", but also for people that were supposedly his friends, but that were getting too close to him, and learning too much about him, and his activities.

He couldn't allow anyone to get that close!

He has many houses in many countries and no one ever knows where he will be at any given time. His main residence, his "pride and joy", was a 2000 acre ranch located outside the city of Pamplona, in the Colombian state of Santander.

Santander is a foggy town, surrounded by high mountains. He had lived there as a child, watching the wild horses free through the dusty country side together, raising clouds of dust wherever they went.

He loved horses so much that he now raises Arabian stallions, and has a herd of over 60 purebred Arabians at his ranch.

He also has a prized collection of fighting bulls, and stages his own bullfights against other bulls owned by cartel members, betting millions of dollars on which one would win in the bull ring.

Fighting, just like killing people, was in his blood, he believed, as it excited him so much. To Marcos, any type of fighting was good. He sometimes beat men to death for the sheer sport of doing it.

He loved going to cockfights whenever and wherever they were held, and had a good collection of fighting cocks also.

He loved putting razor blades on their legs, and watching as they cut each other to pieces when the fought each other, as he loved the sight and smell of fresh blood, human or animal.

He admired the American gangster "Al Capone", and his way of dealing with his enemies.

He liked the style of the way "Capone" dressed, in his suits and snappy two-toned shoes.

He saw himself in "Al Capone", especially for Al's bravado in his crimes he'd pulled.

He always bought all of the latest electronic gadgets that were being invented, especially "spy" toys. He loved them!

He many times pretended in his mind, to be a real secret-agent, like "James Bond (007).

He loves to collect things, especially very expensive things, and has a big collection of American luxury cars, primarily classic automobiles from the past.

His collection includes classic 1933 and 34 Ford coupes, and some roadsters, all in pristine, original condition. He has hot-rods with big, powerful V-8 engines from the 50's through the 70's. Along with them he has Model-T's in mint condition, and almost a dozen Corvettes of the 60's and 70's, both coupes and convertibles.

His favorite motorcycle is a "Harley-Davidson" 750 SPORTSTER, which he loves to ride fast with no helmet, allowing the wind to blow through his hair with his "aviator" sunglasses on.

These expensive, "grown-up" toys cast a lot of money to acquire, especially with the taxes being so high in Colombia. But, money is one thing he has "tons" of, enough to burn bundles of 100 dollar bills in his fireplaces, instead of wood.

His brother, now a "LT." in the Colombian Army, is very well connected in getting the things he wants imparted to him.

His collection of antique and modern firearms rival those of other collectors.

He has customized .357 magnums that are gold-plated, with mother-of-pearl inlays, and .44 magnums with gold-plating and pure hand-carved Ivory handles encrusted with diamonds and emeralds and rubies.

His rifle collection includes both Winchester, Remington and Old Henry lever action repeating rifles of different calibers, most in perfect condition with custom hand-made stocks.

Some of his favorite "toys" are his large collection of cross-bows, and he is an expert marksman with all of the weapons in his collection.

He loves spraying full clips at bowling pins out on his ranch, using either his M-60 machine gun, or his TECH-9's, or maybe his MAC-10's, or any of his UZI's in various calibers, including his favorite .45 caliber INGRAM machine-pistol

Some of his favorite animals are his two beautiful pet wolves out on the ranch. They are perfectly trained, just like guard dogs. They are ferocious looking, and can stare right through you with their large, grey eyes that glow in the dark at night. They once ripped a man apart and partially ate him after he accidently stumbled onto the ranch property several years ago. He laughed about that one, as about all he could find of the man's body was his head and hat.

Marcos knows of so many ways to dispose of bodies, as to leave no evidence of a murders he commits. He usually uses quick-lime to dissolve the flesh and bones down to mush.

Usually around "Christmastime", he likes to dig a large hole about 50 feet wide by 100 feet long by 20 feet deep out on the ranch, like a large swimming pool.

He throws hand grenades, TNT, C-4 plastic explosive, and any other explosives he can locate and buy, into the hole, as he loves the sounds of the explosions, and the vibration of the earth when they go off.

One of his favorite pastimes is chasing and taking to bed beautiful blond-haired, blue-eyed girls between 18-21 years old.

He is always successful when he wants to make love to a woman as they love his free - spending ways with them, with gifts of expensive jewelry, and they love his "Clint Eastwood movie-star good looks too.

It doesn't matter if they are married or not, as he'll still chase them and woo them, fiscally taking them to his bed. He doesn't care if they are virgins or not either, as it is sweeter to him if they are.

He is a sex-addict, and can never get enough of them, always on the prowl for more and more pleasure, no matter what the risk.

One embarrassing trait that he possesses is "kleptomania", as he is always stealing small and easily concealable paintings and knick-knacks, even though he always carries anywhere from five to twenty thousand dollars in his pockets

But, that aside, Marcos is one of the most dangerous men in Colombia, if not the world.

Even though he may smile at you, or shake your hand, or even call you his friend, he is actually thinking when he will kill you, and how he intends to do it.

You do not cross "Marcos" if you want to go on living, because by doing so, you most assuredly won't!

# CHAPTER 4

......................................................

# "The Greatest Surgeon In The World"

As a four year old in "Cali", Colombia, I remember the huge house we lived in, in a middle-class neighborhood. It was right next to a Colombian Air Force Base. Everyone had nice big cars, and big dogs, and nice yards to play in.

The lease was "huge"! It was about two miles wide, and about that long also. As a child, I was amazed at all of the planes there were on the base. I watched them take off and land all the time, and they even flew at night too.

They had fighters, and bombers and lots of helicopters of different sizes.

In "1961" my father was a retired Air Force Mechanic, who at that time, was working for the largest beer company in Colombia, which was "Bavaria".

The director of the company was my "god-father", and his wife was my "god-mother". They were a really nice couple, and were very loving.

The house that we lived in was very large, especially so to a four year old boy. It sat on a large corner lot. It had a big front yard and a large backyard also.

It had a lot of rooms in it, and the largest room belonged to my mom and dad, as their private bedroom.

My room was next to theirs, and my brothers room was right next to mine.

I had everything that I needed there in my room. I had my own bed, my own big clothes closet to hang my clothes up in, and my own dresser drawers and other furniture and some table lamps. It was my own very special private space. I liked it a lot!

My dad taught me very early in life to be really neat in my appearance, and, like a little "soldier", to place my shoes under my bed nice and straight, and keep them shined.

My bed was always to be made with an eight inch collar, and no wrinkles in the sheets or blankets were allowed.

He made sure that my brother and I had a haircut every two weeks without fail, and it was kept "military" style.

He also always made sure we were awake at five-thirty every morning, without fail. Dad didn't believe in "laziness".

Then, after I made my bed and made sure my clothes were laid out for the day, it was "shower time". He always made sure that I scrubbed behind my ears.

After showering, and making sure that my room was clean and neat, it was six o'clock in the morning, and time for breakfast.

We would all sit down at a large, long dinner table together. My favorite breakfast was "Kellogg's Sugar Frosted Flakes" with whole milk, orange juice, and sometimes carrot juice mixed with it.

My Mom and dad sat at each end of the table, and my dad always prayed before each meal, thanking God for our food.

My mom was "Jewish", and she always prepared a lot of "Jewish" foods for us. I really loved her cooking, and always wanted second helpings of everything.

Yet, for being "Jewish", she didn't always adhere to, and practice, all of the "Jewish" laws. She just followed some of the rituals of the faith.

One of my favorite memories is of the big "parrot" that my dad had. I love "parrots"!

His name was "Lorenzo", and he would fly from his "perch", and land on my dad's shoulder whenever he called his name.

Then he would walk his way down my dad's arm, and take his "special" place in front of my dad, right next to his plate at the table in front of him.

Dad would take a bite off of his plate, and "Lorenzo" would then take a bite off of dad's plate, too. But, he never ate anything off of anyone else's plate, just my dad's.

I was very fascinated by "Lorenzo", as I thought that he was the smartest bird in the whole wide world.

My father was a very quiet man, and he was very disciplined and organized in everything that he did, like a big soldier.

He always treated my mom and me, and my brother with lots of respect, and I never ever heard my dad yell or cuss at my mom either.

My dad had a green Ford pick-up truck. It was a 1956 model, I think. It had a 6 cylinder engine in it, and a three-speed manual transmission mounted on the floor.

The three-speed transmission had a rumble and a whine that I still remember, from the gears turning each other around and around.

We had a nice stove, and a big refrigerator in our kitchen that held a lot of food in it. We always had lots of food, and mom would cook a lot, and give pockets of food away every months to people in need.

After we ate our breakfast together, my dad would take my brother and I to a private school, which was a military academy.

Our uniform for the Military Academy was a white shirt, with black pants and suspenders, & black leather shoes. My dad always made sure that our shirts and pants were sharply creased, and that we had shined our shoes really good. He always "inspected" when he dropped us off.

As a child, my dream was to become a doctor when I grew up. I wanted to make people well that were sick. I just knew that with the right medical training from college and a medical school, that I could become the "greatest" surgeon that the world had ever known, and would heal all of the sick people that came to my doctor's office for help.

My brother was always really good with numbers and mathematics, but I don't remember ever hearing him say what he wanted to be when he grew up.

But, I always knew that I wanted to be a "Surgeon", so that I could heal the sick people, and fix whatever was broken.

I told my mom and dad, and everyone I knew, that I would be a great surgeon someday, and they all agreed with me that I would be the best in the world.

Mom and dad always told me that you can become whatever you want to be if you really want it that bad, and study hard in school every day.

I was determined to study hard all the time, and spent most of my time in my "backyard operating room", performing surgeries on my "patients".

Whenever I went to my "operating room" out in the back yard, I would take my "surgical" kit with me to operate on my "patients" with. I created it myself from things I found in our medicine cabinet in the house.

It consisted of a sharp needle and some black thread, and a very sharp double-edged razor blade from my dad's razor in the bathroom, and a bottle of alcohol and some cotton balls that I used to apply the alcohol to my patients with.

I used a wooden board as an "operating" room table. It had four nails in it, one in each corner, to secure my patients to the board, so that they were immobilized and couldn't move.

I was looking for sick people to operate on and make well, but all I could find in my yard were little green lizards, so the lizards became my "people/patients" that I would make well.

When I tried to pick up the lizards, they always ran away from me, as they were searching for some bugs to eat.

I would run after them, and chase them until I caught one, and then I would tie it down onto the operating room table with some string I had in my surgical kit.

I would then take a cotton ball and pour some alcohol on it, and clean the lizards belly with it to disinfect it.

Then, after I prepared the lizard for surgery, I would sterilize the needle and razor blade, which were my surgical instruments. I always did this to make sure that there would be no infections from germs or bacteria.

I would, very carefully, then take my razor blade, which I pretended was my scalpel, and carefully make an "incision" down the lizards tummy, from the neck down to the bottom of its stomach, to what I believed was its umbilical cord.

Of course, I didn't find an umbilical cord, but, since I was pretending he was a human patient, I pretended that he had one, and my "incision" was to where I imagined it would be at.

I would then very carefully spread open the incision and was always really "amazed" at what I found inside my patients.

I was always extremely careful and delicate when I operated on my patients, as I didn't ever want to damage anything inside of them.

I realized even at that age that a doctor is always supposed to use their skills to save lives, and not to cause pain or damage to the patients they are operating on.

After making sure that my patients were ok, and that there were no infections or diseases in its organs, I would take my needle and thread and close up the incision on my patient nice and neatly.

I was then convinced that he was going to be the healthiest and happiest "person/lizard" in the whole world from then on.

I would then untie the strings from the nails on the "operating room" board, and release my "happy," smiling patient.

In my mind, I had just performed an amazing and complicated surgical procedure that only I knew how to do, and I believed that I was the "best" surgical doctor in the whole world. That made me really, really happy!

While the other kids in our neighborhood played football or soccer, or baseball, or any other sports or games, I would be in my backyard, chasing and catching lizards, and practicing my surgical techniques to become "the greatest Surgeon in the World"!

As it sometimes happened, I would be right in the middle of an important, "life saving" surgery on a "patient," and I would be interrupted by my mom calling me to come to eat at the kitchen table.

"Juan Pablo, honey; go wash your hands and come in to eat now"! Mom would say to me.

"But, mom; I'm right in the middle of an important operation"! I would tell her.

"Son, you heard your mother, go wash your hands, right now"! My dad would order me.

"Aw, my hands are always clean, as I wash them all the time before I do my operating on my patients".

Mom and dad would just smile at me, and make me wash them again anyway. They were very proud that their oldest son wanted to be a great surgeon someday.

As life goes on, we always had lots of fun and adventures in my family while I was young in Colombia.

My dad used to take all of us to different places every weekend. Sometimes it was to packs where we had really nice picnics.

He would pick the packs we went to, and other important places, for their history.

A lot of them had really big statues, and my brother and I would ask dad who the statues were of, and why they were important to Colombia. We always had a lot of questions to ask dad about, and he was very happy and pleased to answer them for us, as he wanted us to learn something new at every outing location we went to.

My two favorite places were when we went to the river to go swimming, and mom always brought lots of food to cook for a picnic there.

We would go with my dad, and help him gather up some firewood for the campfire. Mom was always in charge of cooking the food for us, and shooed us all away until the food was ready to eat. Then she'd call us to the picnic area, and dad would say grace for us before we all ate anything.

One of my favorite things was tying the two ends of our "hammock" between two trees, and laying on it all day long.

My second favorite place was a mountain that we went to called "Three Crosses".

We can see the "Three Crosses" mountain from the city, as it is a really tall mountain.

We would always go up to the top of the mountain at "Easter" time every year, as this was a "ritual" of the "Catholic" people, of which my father practiced.

I was always curious as to why people were walking on their knees up the mountain, and why some of them had bloody knees and were also carrying crosses and praying out loud.

Dad explained to me that those people had behaved very badly, and were doing this to attain forgiveness from God, and to regain His love for them. He said that this was their pain and sacrifice to obtain that from God.

In my mind, I believed that our family was perfect in everything that we did, so we didn't ever have to do any of those things that the people on the mountain were doing.

I was seven years old then, and I thought that my dad was perfect in every way. He was my "Idol," as he was the best and most perfect husband to my mom, and the best dad in the whole wide world in my eyes. He was a perfect role model in my eyes, and I wanted to be just like him when I grew up.

What I liked the most about my dad was that he could answer all of the questions that I ever asked him, and I believed that he was the smartest man in the world. I thought he knew everything.

It was about this time that mom and dad told me and my brother that our family of four was going to get larger pretty soon, as mom was pregnant.

After hearing them tell me that, I started wondering where babies came from, and I asked my mom about it.

She told me that a big "happy" bird with a big mouth, called a "stork" brought a baby wrapped in clothes to deliver to people that wanted one.

She said that you could get a boy or a girl delivered to your house if you asked for one.

I left the room after she told me that, and my eyes were really wide. I figured I was a big boy now, and had found out the secret way that mom's get babies.

That is when I came up with a really amazing plan.

I would be able to witness the arrival of the big "stork", and actually see the baby delivered to mom at our house.

I told my brother of my place, and both of us could hardly wait to see the big bird fly to the house and land with mom's new baby, wearing a white diaper.

The traditions of our family require that a "mid-wife" come to the house, and take care of mom's needs.

When the "midwife" was there, they always kept the door closed for some reason, I really didn't know why they did.

Only women were allowed to go into mom's bedroom, and all of us "guys" had to stay outside the room.

So, since we couldn't go into the bedroom to watch the "stork" arrive with the baby, I explained to my brother what the plan was that I had worked up, in detail.

I told him to go watch the front door and the hallway, and that I would go up to the roof.

I then told him that if I see the big stock carrying the baby first, that I would yell to him while it was landing.

Then I told him that if he sees it first, to yell up to the roof at me.

We then heard the midwife say that she saw the baby was on the way, and would soon be here.

I told my brother what she had said, and we both got really "excited".

We took our planned positions at our pasts at the front door and hallway, and on the roof, and waited for the big stock bird to arrive, carrying mom's new baby.

We waited and waited, and watched really good for the stock to arrive.

Then, pretty soon, we heard a baby crying out pretty loud, and the midwife said "here she is! It's a beautiful little girl"!

I got down off of the roof and ran into the house, asking my brother why he didn't tell me when the "stock" arrived with the baby.

He swore to me that he didn't even see a bird fly in with the baby. I told him that I was watching real good up on the roof, and I didn't see a stork come by either.

I then figured out what must have happened.

Mom probably had the bedroom window open, and the "stock" flew in real quick and dropped off the baby, then flew away before we could see it.

We were both disappointed that we hadn't gotten to see the "stock" bring the baby to mom, but when the midwife finally let dad and my brother and I into mom's room, we got to very briefly and very carefully hold our new little sister that they "stock" had brought to her.

She was so pretty and so tiny, and she liked to cry a lot. When I held her for a moment, she threw up on my shirt. I didn't care though, because now I had a little sister to help mom feed and take care of, and I was her big brother, too!

Later on, I asked dad why I didn't see the stock arrive with the baby while I was up on the roof.

He then took me for a ride in his Ford truck, and explained to me where babies really came from.

As he told me, I couldn't believe my ears, and my eyes got really big!

I didn't believe where they actually came from, as it didn't seem possible to me that a baby could come out of something that small.

When we came home, mom was crying because she was so happy, and everyone said to leave her alone to rest.

I went outside in the backyard with my brother, and I told him that babies are not delivered by a big stock.

I told him what dad had told me during our drive in the pick-up, and his eyes got big and he said: "Yuck, no way, you got to be kidding me, Juan Pablo"!

Later, I went to the library and found a book about babies.

Dad was right! No wonder mom was tired.

Then I started thinking:

"Wow"! "I came out of there too!

Then I thought of it as being pretty neat!

# CHAPTER 5

································································

# Abandoned

We win the perfect family. My Mom and Dad, and my brother and little sister and I. I was now 13 years old, and getting bigger.

Everything was wonderful! My brother and I were going to school at the Military Academy, Mom was at home taking care of my little sister, and dad was working hard at the brewery.

All seemed normal at home, and I had not seen anything wrong, or out of the ordinary in any way. I was unaware of any problems that mom and dad may have had behind their closed bedroom door, but evidently there had been some problems between them.

I had never seen my mom crying about anything, that I could remember. I had never seen her with any black eyes, or a bloody nose, or anything like that. I had never ever known that my mom and dad had ever been fighting about anything. They never even yelled at each other.

But later, I found out that mom was a very jealous and possessive person.

To me, my mom was just a regular "Jewish" mother who cooked and loved and cared for her family. I didn't think of that as special or anything, as she was always very loving and caring to all of us. She was our mom.

I look at her love for us as profound, as it was unconditional love, day in and day out.

I remember it so clearly, as it was just like any other day when he walked out of our lives. Just like that he was gone.

I was sitting in the kitchen eating a piece of toast, and all of the sudden mom started crying. At first she cried softly, and then she was crying uncontrollably, with large tears running down her face.

It was like something unexpectedly dramatic had happened to her, and I didn't know what was happening to her, or why.

I wanted to ask her what was the matter, what was it that happened, but I really didn't know how to ask her that.

I felt so confused, as I saw that she was hurt about something, and at first I thought that maybe it was something that I had done.

But then, suddenly, mom turned and looked at me with big tears on her face. Her eyes were really red, and she dropped the bomb that blew my perfect world to pieces.

"Juan Pablo, your dad has left us"!

"He's gone, hon, and he's not coming back"!

Even though I was just 13 years old, I suddenly felt like I was one hundred.

I felt so empty inside at that moment, as if all of my happiness and future plans had flown away from me. I couldn't become a doctor now.

My future as the "greatest surgeon in the world," and the futures of my mom, and 2 brothers and 2 sisters as well, was suddenly in doubt. Our future as a "family" was in doubt also.

The "castle" that I had been building on the beach of "life" come crashing down as the waves of family tragedy came down on top of everything, destroying my dreams in the process.

I was so full of questions that I needed to ask, but there were no answers for me.

I felt at that moment when mom said dad was gone, and never coming back, that I did not even have a future.

In "shock", I asked mom how this could happen to us, and why had it happened!

My dad was the source of everything in our house, and in our "lives"!

He was the very foundation of our family, and now he was gone from our life.

Mom said that, without dad working and paying the bills, that we could no longer afford to live in our house anymore, and would have to rent a room somewhere.

All of the sudden the enormity of dad leaving us forever hit me, and it felt like I was starting to bubble inside, and I started shaking. Memories started flooding my mind.

I ran out to our backyard, and thought of all my patients that I needed to practice on, and realized I'd never get to make the sick one's well again. It made me hurt so much inside I couldn't stand up any longer.

I fell to my knees on the ground, and the tears started coming and wouldn't stop. My nose started running, but I didn't care anymore, as I didn't have a daddy to love me.

I cried out with my broken heart through my tears; "Dad, dad, please come back, I love you, we all love you, please, please come home"! "I'll be good, dad, we all will"! I cried out. "Daddy, please come home, please"!

But it was no use, as only silence followed my tearful cries.

Mom sold "Lorenzo", my dad's parrot, to someone that day. It hurt me so much that I could feel my heart breaking into a million tiny pieces as I watched him go out the front door.

"What are we going to do now"? I thought!

The next day, mom started selling everything in the house that wouldn't fit in the single room that she had rented for us. A car came that day, and mom sold everything that we couldn't fit into the rented room. She sold it for rent money, and to buy food for us to eat.

At that moment, I began developing an intense hatred for the first time in my life. I had always loved and respected my daddy, but now I could only feel bitterness and hostility toward him for what he had done to us by leaving to be with another woman.

For the first time in my life, I experienced rejection, and I couldn't cope with the emotional upheaval brought on by my dad abandoning us like he did.

I had thought my dad loved my mom and us kids, but he no longer did anymore, as he wanted to be with another woman now.

I took one last look at my bedroom, now empty and devoid of any furniture, and I felt numb inside. I went to the closet and took down my old shoe box that contained my surgical kit. I held it in my hands, like I was trying to hold onto a dream that was slipping away from me. As I opened the lid, memories came to me of the "magical" operations that I had dutifully performed on my many "patients", and the realization that I could no longer practice my surgical techniques in our old backyard anymore. I could no longer heal the sick and make them well again.

I then sat down on the bare floor, and burst into tears as I looked at my "scalpel" and operating room board, and the alcohol bottle and cotton balls I had used for so long in wanting to heal the sick patients I had found.

I crumpled into a heap on the floor and cried uncontrollably until I started to hiccup so much I could hardly breathe anymore.

After what seemed like hours, I finally got up slowly, and picked up my surgical kit, and took it out to the backyard, where I placed it in our trash can and set the trash on fire.

As I watched the box begin to burn, I saw in the flames my intense hatred for my dad begin to intensify, and as the hatred got stronger and stronger, I lost all love and respect that I'd ever had for my dad.

We ended up moving to another house to live that mom had rented a room in. The house was just like our house, in a middle-class neighborhood. It belonged to one of our family's relatives, my grandma's sister.

It had lots of flowers in nice flower beds all around it outside, and my grandma's sister had a lot of potted plants hanging in the house too. The house felt like a monastery, and we were supposed to act like "Monks"!

Mom kept telling us to be very quiet, and to never touch any of the plants, but we did just the opposite of what she told us to do.

We made lots of noise all the time, and destroyed a lot of the plants around the house too, like young boys horse playing will, and when mom came home, after being gone all day and most of the night, our Aunt Rachel told her we were rebellious, incorrigible, uncontrollable, and that mom needed to find another place for us to live as soon as possible, as she couldn't take it anymore.

I had started hating Aunt Rachel for the way she treated us while we lived there, and I hated just about everything in my life at that time.

I was just full of hate because of dad leaving, and abandoning us the way he did, and I didn't care anymore about anything.

One day mom came home with a loading truck, and said we were moving. I was so glad to be getting away from there, as I couldn't play with my friends, or anything. We had been at Aunt Rachel's for about three months, and it had seemed like three years of "hell"!

Mom said that she had found a place with another room that we could rent. It was in another middle class neighborhood. It was a big house, with a nice yard too.

They had a lot of other kids there, boys and girls that were about our age. We had a lot of fun running around the house and playing "hide and seek", and other fun games. We compared our belly-buttons! Some of us had "innies", and some had "outies". My mom shared the kitchen with the other family that lived there, and cooked our meals for us.

The other family that lived in the house had a business. They made nice furniture, like chairs, tables, sofas and loveseats to sell.

We helped them sand down the wood, glue it together, stain it, and put the pieces together. I liked it a lot. It was kind of "fun"!

One day I was watching the lady that owned the house, and I noticed that she had a small wooden box that was shaped like a heart. I saw that the box had a little hole in the top of it, and I watched her drop coins into it every day.

I then noticed where she was hiding the box at, and started thinking about the coins inside the box.

A little while later, I found out that my mom was working for some rich people in their houses, working clothes for them, and stuff like that.

Whenever she came home, she would be carrying some plastic bags that had leftover food in them that the rich people didn't eat.

I felt bad when I saw my mom doing that, as it was humiliating to me that other people saw that we were eating stuff that rich people were going to throw in the trash.

After watching the lady put coins in the little box for weeks, I wondered how many coins were in the box one day.

I had never stolen anything in my whole life, but that day I thought of how much few I could have with some coins, maybe to go to a movie with, at the movie theater. I could take someone with me, if they would keep it a secret.

This was the very first criminal act of my life.

I waited until everyone was really busy, and no one was looking. I got the little box from the lady's hiding place, and snuck out the back door of the house, going to a wooded area nearby.

I found a big rock on the ground, and I smashed it against the box until it broke in little bitty pieces and the coins spilled out of it.

I picked up the coins and put them in my pants pockets. There were a lot of them in the little box, as it had been almost full.

I invited one of my brothers to go to the movies with me, to see a really good monster movie.

I bought a pack of Marlboros cigarettes, and for the first time, began smoking in the shadows of the theater that day.

I went to the concession stand and got us some potato chips, buttered popcorn, chocolate covered raisins, chocolate covered peanuts, some large candy bars, some cakes, some pretzels, jelly beans, and other stuff to eat while we watched "Godzilla" destroy Tokyo, Japan!

After the movie, we came home late in the afternoon that day. Mom was madder than I had ever seen her in my whole life.

She demanded to know which one of us had taken the coin box. I denied doing it, but my brother got really scared, and told her that I did it, and that I had spent the coins to take us to the movies.

Then she called me into the room that we rented in the house, and locked the door behind us.

My mom then become a monster that was even worse than "Godzilla"!

Mom's anger and frustration that she had been building up since my dad left just exploded, and she began taking it out on me for taking the coin box.

She started beating me like she wanted to kill me, first with her hands, and then with a broom stick. I tried to get away from her, but I finally gave up and just curled up on the floor as she kept on hitting me again and again, after she knocked me down.

My brothers and sisters had heard all the yelling and noise coming from our room, and they had come running. They were outside the door, but couldn't get in because the door was locked.

They started yelling really loud that mom was killing me.

Mom took the broomstick and put it on my throat, putting a foot at one end of the stick, and pressed down on my throat with the other end, like she was trying to choke me to death with it.

I was so scared, and I felt like I was dying as she pushed the stick down harder and harder on my throat.

There was a four inch gap under our door, and my brothers and sisters were watching it happen. They thought she was really going to kill me that day.

They started crying out desperately for help, saying:

"She's gonna kill Juan Pablo, mom's gonna kill him"!

Finally, the oldest son of the owner of the house came, and he used his shoulder to knock the door down. He screamed at my mom to stop, but she acted like she didn't hear him.

She was acting like she had went insane, and he had to physically pull my mom off of me.

After everyone had calmed down, I felt so guilty for having taken the coin box.

I felt that what I had done had justified my mom's anger, and her actions towards me that day.

It wasn't long after that, that my grandma came to see my mom, and grandma asked her to send me and my brother to her house.

Grandma said that she was going to start a pastry business, and that she needed our help to sell her pies to support the business.

So my brother and I were sent over to my grandma's house to help her sell pies.

My Grandma lived in an old "Ghetto" neighborhood, where all of the houses were old and broken down, and ugly looking.

The people that lived in the ghetto loved my grandma very much, and watched out for her. She was welcomed with open arms when she moved there.

She lived there with her sister, "Elvita and her mother, "Ellen", who was one hundred years old. I never realized that people could get that old.

They worked together sewing and making clothes for the prostitutes that worked in the neighborhood.

It was then that for the first time in my life that I really started to take notice of the kinds of people that lived around my grandma. They kind of acted weird.

There were prostitutes, whore houses, thieves drug pushers, alcoholics, killers, and all different kinds of street people living in the area around 13TH ST. where grandma lived.

I felt like I was on another "planet"!

For the first-time, I was exposed to a world that had been unknown to me while I was a child growing up in middle-class neighborhoods.

This was the "real" world I was in now, and I was both scared, and at the same time, fascinated by the people I met there.

My grandma made all kinds of pastries and pies, and my brother and I went around the neighborhood ghetto and helped her sell them.

We'd tell everyone we met how good a cook our grandma was, and how sweet the pastries and pies were. We'd say:

"Our grandma makes the best pies and pastries in the whole wide world, and all you gotta do is take just one bite and you'll see"!

Lots of people took our word for it, and bought grandma's pastries, and she sold all of the pies she made. Grandma would then help mom out with money.

I soon found out that I had something in common with the street people in the ghetto.

Like me, some of them had no mother or father, and some of them had nothing to their name, and no one at all to love or care about them.

A lot of them had been in and out of prison several times, and I was hanging around with them.

I started stealing things at every available opportunity

My mom found out about my thefts, and she started beating me again.

The beatings became more intense, as she was trying to change me from my criminal ways.

She'd beat me with just about anything she could get her hands on at the time.

I became very resentful, and I started hating my mom, while at the same time I loved her. I didn't ever realize before then that you could both love someone, and hate them at the same time. It made me feel confused.

One of the street people, a criminal, gave me a manicure set to sell. I sold it and kept the money. The next day I lied to him and told him that the police had taken it away from me. He didn't believe me.

He punched me on the left side of my face then, really hard, as he was angry at me.

"butcher"

I ran and got a knife out of my grandma kitchen, and I chased him down the street till he disappeared down an alley.

Someone then said that the cops were coming, and one of the prostitutes came and took the knife, and hid me in her house to protect me from the police.

The prostitute said that I was really day. That made me feel kind of grown up, and I felt like I was starting to become a real man.

I started going over to the prostitutes house every day. I would eat there sometimes, and smoke cigarettes, and maybe drink a few beers with her.

She started teaching me about sex, and how to pleasure and satisfy a woman, and I learned real quick. We practiced every chance we could, and I became what she called "a real stud"!

She encouraged me in my stealing, and told me that I would be a real pro someday, what she called "a professional criminal. She said that I had real ability as a thief, pushed me to practice and get better at it.

We talked a lot when I spent time at her house, and I found out that some of her brothers were criminals.

They sold drugs, and stole anything and everything that they could lay their hands on.

But, she said that I was different, and she encouraged me a lot, as she wanted me to become a professional criminal. She said I was not only smart, but that I was becoming what she called "street smart"!

We'd been at grandma's for about a year, and one evening I was sitting at the dinner table eating. I was then 14 years old.

I heard my grandma's voice at the front door, and wondered who was talking to her.

Grandma then said "Azucena, look at what I have here", to my mom!

Everyone then ran to the front door, my mom and my brothers and sisters. Once they saw who was standing there, they became really excited.

I looked out from the kitchen door, and tried to see what all of the excitement was about, and then I saw him standing by the door.

My dad had returned home, after having been gone for over a year! He was standing in the doorway, leaving on a pair of crutches. He said that he had fallen and broken his leg.

My mom, and my brothers and sisters all rushed to him, and began hugging and kissing him a lot!

He noticed that I had held back, and hadn't rushed to the door with them to greet him.

I was so angry that he had left us the year before, and I now hated my dad for abandoning us like that.

I didn't care if he ever returned home, as I no longer loved or respected him.

All that he had with him were the pair of crutches. No suitcase, no money, no gifts for mom or any of us, nothing. I shouted "I hate you, I hate you," as I ran back into the kitchen!

He moved back in with us, and slept with mom again, and acted as though he had never left us. That made me even angrier at him, and I made up my mind about him.

I let him know how I felt by the way I acted towards him, and my behavior.

I disobeyed everything he told me, and rebelled against him, totally disregarding his parental authority. I no longer respected him or loved him after what he had done to us, and I no longer recognized him as my boss at home.

He began using any excuse that he could come up with to beat me up. He used wire, electrical cables, wooden 2x4's, belts, anything he could get his hands on.

He finally started using the flat pact of a machete knife blade to beat me with, when he saw that nothing else was working.

Another way that he punished me was to get a cord from the kitchen.

He would tie both of my feet at the ankles, and pull me up by my feet to the ceiling, using a wooden beam to support me. I was suspended upside down from the ceiling rafters, with my head about two feet above the floor.

He would light a fire of newspapers under me, and the flames from it would burn my hair, and my head and neck and shoulders. I was so filled then with hate for him that I wanted to kill him.

One night, after he had been beating me, he took a rope that he had, and tied my hands behind my back, and tied me to a post that we had in the back yard. Then he tied my ankles to the bottom of the post, and put some rope around my neck and tied it to the post also.

He left me there until two o'clock in the morning, until my mom came outside and untied me finally.

My brother and I really loved cocoa. One time soon after, he and I ate all of the Nestlé's Quick cocoa mix from the kitchen.

Mom demanded to know who had ate all of it, and my brother, really scared, told her that "I did it"!

My mom then took me to the stove, and put my hands on top of the stove burners, burning my hands and making big blisters on them.

I took off running then, screaming from the intense pain from my hands, with the skin hanging off of my fingers.

Mom then chased me down with a giant tube of toothpaste, putting some all over my hands and fingers, as she thought it would help with the pain, and stop me from screaming so loud.

"It did not help at all"!

After that, she got really mad at me for something that I did, and took me to the laundry room, filled a tub with water, and held my head underwater until I thought I was going to drowned.

Very soon after that, I stated some money from my dad's pants pocket, and I ran away from home.

I stayed gone for about a year, and finally returned home when I was almost 16!

Soon after my sixteenth birthday, I was becoming incorrigible and uncontrollable living at home. Then, an amazing thing then happened one morning at about 6 am., several months later.

My mom started screaming really loud, and I ran into her bedroom to see what was the mother with her!

All of my brothers and sisters came running also, to see why she was screaming!

When we asked her what was the matter, she said "Your father is dead"!

He had been coughing up a lot of blood for awhile, and had died of cirrhosis of the liver.

He had been a really bad alcoholic most of his life, and it had finally caught up with him.

I felt nothing inside when he died, as it was as if I no longer had any emotional feelings in me besides hate and anger at him.

Soon I became a real delinquent, and was drinking all the time, using drugs, staying out all night, stealing anything that I could find to get money for drugs, and starting to become a real criminal. In my mind, I needed training in weapons to become a real professional criminal, so I decided to join the Colombian Army. I needed the paperwork anyway for working.

# CHAPTER 6

# Weapons Training

When I turned seventeen years old I altered my birth certificate to show that I was eighteen, so that I could join the Colombian Army.

In Colombia, if you want to get a good job, you need to show that you've served in the Armed Forces of your country.

On February 16, 1974 I went into the Colombian Army, as I wanted to become the most "highly trained" soldier in the world. But little did I know that when I left my family to go for basic training, that I would never see my mother alive again.

We all went down to one of the large Army bases, where I was to board a military bus that would take me to my training camp. My mother and grandmother, and my two brothers and two sisters all came to see me off. They all kept hugging me and kissing me, and telling me how very proud they were of me. That made me very happy!

I had tears in my eyes as I picked up my suitcase and got on board the army bus, where I took a seat all the way to the back.

I looked out the back window and saw my mom and younger siblings waving at me.

The bus then started pulling away from the base, and all of them started running behind the bus, waving and crying out to me;" I Love you, Juan Pablo"; with tears streaming down their faces.

I burst into tears as I looked out the back window at them, and cried like a baby as the bus sped up and left them farther and farther behind us, until they were lost behind the huge cloud of dust kicked up off of the old rotted dirt road.

As I watched them disappear in the distance, I had no idea of the heartbreak I would feel in just a matter of several weeks.

On April 3rd, barely six weeks after I had arrived at my training camp, I was summoned to my commanders office. He informed me that there was a situation at home with my family, and that I was needed there immediately.

He then ordered me to store my military arms and equipment, and take leave on the next available bus back home.

As I rode the military bus back towards "Medellin", I had so many different ideas of what may be wrong going through my head I could hardly think straight. What could have happened to cause me to be needed so badly?

As I got off the bus in Medellin, I had a bad feeling that something was terribly wrong at home, but I just couldn't figure out what it could be. As I hailed a taxi, I hoped that it wasn't too bad.

As I arrived at my grandmother's house and exited the cab, I could see my brothers and sisters, my grandmother and other relatives, along with some friends and neighbors, out in front of the house. They were crying hard, with tears running down their faces.

As I approached the house, they looked up and saw me, and came running towards me. My sweet grandma came up to me and tearfully said; "Juan Pablo, your mother is dead"!

I was in shock, as at first the words wouldn't register in my brain, as I kept thinking "No, that can't be true, mom is too young to die"! "She's only 42 years old"!

"What are we going to do, Juan Pablo"? my brothers and sisters cried out, as they hugged me tightly, seeking guidance about a future they were now unsure of. I felt numb as I walked toward the house, not knowing really what to expect.

As I walked in the front door, the crowd of friends, relatives and well wishers made room for me, and parted like the Red Sea as I went towards the living room.

It was then that I saw her, lying in repose in a dark brown casket in the center of the room.

I just stood there, and looked at her face for I don't really know how long. It was as though I couldn't tear myself away from her

I ached inside, and felt so empty. I loved my mother so much, and now for some reason she had been taken away from me forever.

In my mind, I kept asking the question over and over again: "What kind of God would let this happen"? "She was so young, only 42"!

I slowly walked up to the casket, feeling as if I weighed a thousand pounds and could barely make my body move forward.

As I gently raised the clear glass upper lid of the coffin, I noticed that my mom was wearing one of my favorite shirts.

It was then that the memory of what she had said just before I left for my training flooded into my mind, and brought tears to my eyes.

She had said that she wanted to be buried in one of my shirts, as she knew that she would never see her "Juan Pablo" again.

As the heavy tears from my eyes began streaming down my cheeks, I slowly bent down and kissed her tenderly on the forehead.

It was at that moment, that for the first time in my life I felt the coldness of death! The effect it had came at that moment was tremendous and immediate.

The pain going through me was so great that I could not bring myself to go with everyone else to the cemetery for my mother's burial, as I knew that I would not be able to stand to see the ground where she was to be buried, nor be able to watch as dirt was laid on top of the coffin.

I stayed behind, and stared out the window as I watched the rest of my family and friends drive away to attend the burial.

As they left the house, there was an explosion of emotions going on inside of me. Stronger and more powerful than I had ever felt in my life!

It was "hate!" Hate to the darkest extent that I had ever felt before, towards both God and humanity.

I believe that on that day my human, fleshly heart was forcefully ripped out of my chest, and replaced with cold, hard granite stone that had no "heartbeat."

Then, I realized that now, more than ever before, that I needed to become "the best trained soldier in the world!"

But, now I had another reason for the training, as I now wanted to become the most highly trained "criminal" in the world!

At that moment, I both despised and rejected all of the "good" advice that my mom had given to me, and I swore to myself that I refuse to live and die as a poor man.

Returning to the base several days later, I continued my training with even more dedication, focus and zeal, learning all that I could about all the weapons at my disposal. I became an expert marksman using the M-16 A1 assault rifle, the M-60 heavy machine gun, M-79 and M-203 grenade launchers, .45 caliber automatic pistol, and even the .50 caliber "sniper" rifle that used the best high powered scope made.

The sniper rifle became my favorite weapon of choice after the machine guns. I practiced with it daily, becoming highly proficient at hitting targets at great distances; 500-750-1000 yards away.

My Lt. Commander noticed my dedication, and approached me on a Saturday morning as I practiced my different firing positions at the range.

"Castillo, why aren't you off base enjoying your weekend of liberty?" asked the Lt.

"I am getting in more practice time with the sniper rifle, sir"! I answered him.

"Castillo, I commend your dedication to duty, and your extra marksmanship practice hours, but the Sgt. tells me you've been here three weekends in a row now, and I seriously think you should take a break from your training and relax a little and have some fun"! the Lt. says to Juan Pablo.

"Ok Lt., if you insist, sir"! replies Juan Pablo.

I then unloaded, cleaned, and then oiled the sniper rifle, and turned it back in to the company armory, replacing the scope in its cushioned box.

– – – – – – – – – – – – – – – – – –

I was almost done with my two year enlistment when I was called into the office of my Commanding Officer. He said to me:

"Castillo, you have the finest record of anyone on this base, and have mastered all small arms to the extent that you qualify as an expert. "We need men like you to teach other soldiers how to fight! Will you consider staying in the Army, and becoming an instructor to the new recruits"?

"I have been thinking about that, sir, and I appreciate your asking me to stay, but there are many pressing problems that I need to be tending to at home". I answered.

"Well, at least think about it, Castillo. You would make us a fine arms instructor"! he replied.

I actually had considered staying in the military, but had decided against it after my mother died. Since she was gone, I had lost all inspiration to be a professional soldier.

Upon finishing my two year enlistment, I returned home to Medellin, and moved back in with my grandmother. She loved me like my mother did, and always cooked a lot of food and pastries for me to eat.

After my mother had passed away, my two brothers and two sisters were split up among other relatives of ours. But, I still saw them as much as I could, when I could.

After moving back in with grandma, I found a job as a Security Officer for a bank there in Medellin. I liked working there a lot, especially watching the bank tellers count the big piles of money from the vault every day.

While working there at the bank, I ended up meeting the women of my dreams! "Martha"!

She was so very "beautiful and elegant"! At about 5'8" inches tall, she was much shorter than I am, what I'd call a perfect fit.

I loved "everything" about her!

From her dark brown brunette hair that tumbled down her back and over her shoulders, to her clear olive colored complexion and mysterious dark brown eyes, she was perfect in every way.

She had the most beautiful face that I have ever seen on a woman, even without putting on any make-up.

She was "full busted", and it was well impossible for any man to turn away after looking at her passing by.

She reminds me of the actress of the "Desperate Housewives" television show, only she was even more "refined and alluring," and so very "enticing". Territory Hatcher had nothing on her!

I had fell in love with her from the very first moment I laid eyes on her, and she readily accepted my invitation out to dinner and dancing.

Watching her out on the "disco" dance floor was mesmerizing, as she moved like she'd been born on one.

Many times we went on long walks along country roads, listening to the birds chirp as they took flight, and enjoyed the serenity of the quiet mornings as the gentle winds were blowing through the trees, rustling the colorful leaves.

We made love countless times under the night skies, with only the bright shining stars as our blanket.

We were so much in love, and for three years we lived together in my apartment, sharing our thoughts and dreams with each other. I had never been so happy in my life, as she meant everything to me.

I was ready to settle down, I felt. I had been secretly shopping around at several jewelry stores, trying to find her the perfect diamond engagement ring, as I wanted to surprise her by asking her to marry me, and be mine forever.

But it was not to be, as one evening over dinner, she gently told me that I needed to find a woman that could love me as much as I loved her.

I felt my heart breaking into countless pieces, as I realized then that she was leaving me. She said:

"Juan Pablo, you need to find a good woman that will love you, and stand by your side, as I don't deserve you".

I tearfully asked her "why", but she just softly kissed me, got up from the table, and walked out the door with her suitcases, and out of my life.

She was used to having the "finest" things in life, things that I could not provide her, especially on a bank Security Officers salary.

At that moment my hatred at the world intensified, and I swore that I would never again lose a woman because of a lack of money.

I swore to myself that no matter what it took, I would become a "rich man", and never have to want for material things.

For weeks after she left I was in so much emotional pain that I locked myself inside my apartment with nothing but bottles of liquor and music, alone and away from everyone.

What kept going through my mind, over and over again, was that the reason she had left me was because I'm "poor", I'm literally "broke"!

That was when I made up my mind that, no matter what, I will make lots of money, and she "will" see me again!

But, I refused to allow her to see me live from "paycheck to paycheck"!

When I pulled myself together, I went to a bar that I knew, where I could connect with some criminal contacts.

After several weeks of hanging out there, I met a man called "Mario". I told him that I was looking for a way to make lots of money, and I told him about my military training.

He told me that he knew some people, and would get back to me in a few days.

Within three days he came back to me, and said that he had some people who wanted to meet with me.

That night he took me to a bar called "NUTU VARA", in a really famous hotel in "Medellin". The bar was located in the back.

He then introduced me to four men. Their names were "Swede, Ernesto, Nelson and Jonathan".

Swede said to me; "Mario told us that you want to roll with us to make some money".

I answered; "Yes, I do"! I then explained to him my desire to make a lot of money, and why I didn't care anymore how I did it! "Swede" then said: "I think we can work something out".

Then he and the other three men reached into their pockets and pulled out big wads of cash, and each of them handed me a large chunk of money in big bills.

They told me to go buy some nice clothes and pay bills, and that they would see me the following week.

About a week later, I met with them again, and they took me to a lumber yard that had lots of building materials.

They pretended to be customers as I was shown where the office was.

"Swede" said: "There is a check for two hundred and fifty pesos in the desk, and I need you to go into the office and get it for me"!

That would be my mission, to retrieve the check for him.

We left and went out to dinner at a fancy restaurant, eating steaks and drinking fine wines.

The next day "Swede" handed me a .357 magnum "Python", and told me to go with "Ernesto", and retrieve the check for him.

In my mind, I was thinking that this was my opportunity to show these professionals what I am capable of.

As "Ernesto" and I drove back to the lumber yard, I pulled out the .357 magnum and checked the cylinders to make sure it was loaded. I placed it back in my waistband and covered it with my light jacket, concealing it.

As we arrived at the lumber yard, "Earnesto" backed the car into a parking stall to make our getaway easier when we left.

Once inside, I pulled my "messenger of death", the .357, out of my waistband and "Ernesto" pulled out his pistol also!

But it was me that was giving the orders to the lumber yard employees, as I waved the "Python" in their direction! I said.

"If you don't want to die, do exactly as I say, and follow my orders! Don't do anything stupid because I won't hesitate to kill you if you try!"

"All of you, get into the back room, now!"

They all quietly obeyed my orders.

I then closed the door behind them and locked it securely.

Immediately I ran into the office and began searching for the check, looking through everything I could find. "Nothing"!

I searched and I searched for the check, but I could not find it anywhere in the office, and I began to get very frustrated.

"Let's go"; Ernesto said to me, as he placed his pistol back into his shoulder holster.

I looked at him, puzzled that he wanted to leave before I found the check for "Swede".

To my way of thinking, this didn't make sense, and it raised many doubts and questions in my mind, because this mission, this "operation", was a "failure".

I felt confused as we got in the car and left, going back to meet with the others, feeling that I had failed them by not being able to retrieve the check.

I wondered what they would think of me, now that I had failed to bring back the check to them.

As we arrived and got out of the car, I started walking toward "Swede", who was standing with Nelson and Jonathan.

As we approached them, I started to explain that the check wasn't in the office, but before I could say anything, "Ernesto" smiled at "Swede" and said

"He did good! He handled himself like a man who knows what he's doing. He's "OK" by me, Swede"!

I then realized that this had been a "test" to see if I had the brains and courage to get a job done. I had "passed", and as they all smiled at me, they said that it was also my initiation into the group.

That was how they welcomed me as a member of the "Wind Fleet"!

After joining them, I began going with them on many bank robberies, and in getting my cut of the money, made me a millionaire.

I had never seen, nor held in my hands, as much money as I now had. Stacks and stacks of large bills, and all mine to spend!

About four months after joining the "Wind Fleet", I was told by the owner of the house where I rent my apartment that I was wanted on the phone.

I went into her living room and picked up the phone, thinking that maybe it was "Swede" calling to have me meet them someplace for a job.

But before I could get the phone to my ear, my landlady said:

"Guess who it is"?

I just looked at her, not knowing what she was trying to say.

"It's Martha"! she cried out excitedly!

Happiness then flooded my head as the sweet memories filled my mind of the time we had spent together.

I screamed out "Yesssss! Alright"!

My mind was working quickly as I thought of what to say to her.

Now that my pockets were "bulging" with cash, I was going to show her that she had made a big mistake by leaving me.

I picked up the phone and said:

"Hello"!

She then said "Hello Baby"!

I was so excited and happy to hear her voice again, I was at a loss for words for a moment as my mind raced ahead of my actions.

"OH Martha, Honey! I thought I'd never hear from you again"! I replied to her.

"Well, Juan Pablo, I've been pretty busy these days. I hear you're doing good, honey!"

"Yes, things have gotten much better for me in the past few months, and business is good. How have you been doing, beautiful"!?

"Guess what, baby? our dream came true"!

"What do you mean"?

"I'm pregnant, darling! and it's yours"!

Hearing her say these words literally knocked me off my feet, to say the least.

"OH my darling, this makes me so happy"! I said, as I sat down on a couch then got back up again, being so excited I couldn't sit still

"Where are you, hon"? I asked her as I picked up a pen and paper.

"I'm in Armenia, baby, about 500 miles from "Medellin"! Can you come to see me"?

"I'll be there as soon as possible, hon"; I said to her, as she gave me the address where she was living and hung up the phone.

I was so happy that I didn't even want to go to the airport to get a flight.

I just packed all of my good clothes into my suitcases, and included about $ 1.5 million dollars I had stashed in my closet in another suitcase.

I called a taxi, and when he arrived I told him if he'll drive me to Armenia, Colombia, I'll pay him whatever he wanted.

I gave him $5,000.00 cash as advance payment, which made him very very "happy"!

We arrived at the address in Armenia the next morning, and I found out then that Martha was living with her mother, in a house her mother owned.

As I came to the door and knocked, her mom opened the door, gave me a big hug, and welcomed me into the house.

After I came in, and her mother closed the front door, "Martha" came walking out of one of the rooms.

As she entered the living room, I stood up. She kept looking at me from top to bottom, over and over again, noticing my new clothes, new shoes, my cologne, and everything about me.

"Wow, you look different, Juan Pablo"! she said, as she smiled broadly!

Then I said "Yes, and you look very pregnant too, Martha"!

We both then started laughing as we hugged and kissed each other for the first time in 4 months!

I then told her that we're going to a store where they sell maternity clothes and baby clothes, and bassinettes, so that we can get ready for the baby's arrival.

The next day we went shopping, and I spent thousands and thousands of dollars on clothes for both her, and the baby.

After we came back from the baby store, I told Martha to start looking for us a house to live in.

Pretty soon, my sister "Luz" heard of my plans, and told me she needed to talk to me about something.

She then told me that she hadn't wanted to say anything, but now that she'd heard that I was going to buy a house for Martha, she felt that she needed to tell me something she felt I needed to know about.

"Juan Pablo, I hadn't wanted to tell you, as I thought you might do something to Martha. But, when I heard you're giving her a house, I feel I have to tell you".

"Tell me what"? I asked Luz.

"Juan Pablo, after Martha broke up with you, she started living with another man like they were married. The baby is very probably his, hon"!

My sister must have talked to Martha before I had a chance to get to her mother's house, as both she and her lover disappeared that day from Armenia.

So, instead of giving the house to Martha, I gave it to my sister, "Luz".

After this "fiasco", it was reinforced in my mind that I could not trust anyone.

# CHAPTER 7

# "Bad Boys"

## The Members Of "The Wind Fleet"

Marcos

Jonathan

Swede

Adrian

German

Juan Pablo

Alex

# "MARCOS"

(COVER) –      Professional Photographer & Auto parts retailer
(Nickname) –      The "Arranger"
(Description) –      Looks like "Clint Eastwood", 6'2" 215 lbs. curly brown hair.
(Criminal Record)      None – Has never been arrested

### (Background Information)

Marcos is a welcomed associate of the leader of the "Medellin" Cartel, "Pedro Diaz".

He is "highly respected as a man that can arrange to get anything done.

He can arrange for deliveries of drugs and automatic weapons to anywhere in the world.

He takes photographs of area around the robbery location to plan the getaway route.

He is two-faced and a liar, and we'll talk about people behind their back.

He is a "kleptomaniac" that steals small "knick-knacks", even though he carries thousands of dollars.

He is a "cold-blooded" killer that will kill you in a "heartbeat," and one of the highest paid killers in the "Cartel".

# "JONATHAN"

(COVER) –         Auto parts retailer & auto repair
(NICKNAME) -    "El pimpollo"
(Description)      5'4" 220 lbs. of pure "fat"! 36 years old, blue eyes, red hair, pudgy complexion, short stubby fingers.
(Criminal Record) Has been locked up numerous times for various offenses.

### (Background Information)

Lives in an expensive house in a fancy "upscale" neighborhood with a wife and two children. He is an "extrovert," and is always clowning around with practical jokes on others.

Both his wife and mother-in-law support him, as he blows his own money earned from the "Cartel" on his drug and alcohol habits.

He is known by members of the "Medellin" Drug Cartel as a man that can make things happen in the criminal underworld.

He lives to party, and gives the appearance of being very rich. He dresses well also, and loves fancy clothes, expensive cars, cologne, etc.

He loves to chase beautiful women for sex.

He is a very good actor, as when confronted about information that he's been saying things about you, he'll get very emotional and sensitive, and will start crying, asking you how you could ever think anything bad about him.

He is not a "cold-blooded" killer like the other members of the gang, as he has to be plied with drugs and alcohol first, then coerced into doing the killing. He is none the less deadly while on drugs.

# "SWEDE"

| | |
|---|---|
| (COVER) | Auto parts retailer and auto repair |
| (Nickname) | "BOSTON" |
| (GANG Position) | Leader – Bank Robbery Leader (Overall Manager) |
| (Description) | 49 yrs. Old, 5'9" tall, 185 lbs. brown hair, white complexion, green eyes. |
| (Disposition) | Is very organized and professional in both his criminal activities and his personal life. |

(Criminal Record) –Has been incarcerated before on various charges.

## (Background)

He lives with his two sisters in their mid-forties in a fancy house, yet he has a very beautiful wife, and many girlfriends, that he has living in other expensive houses in other locations.

All of his houses are full of expensive antiques and porcelain items.

His sisters take care of his house he lives in.

He loves fancy, expensive cars and weapons.

He is highly intelligent, and a good conversationalist.

He loves good food and gambling.

He is very adept at obtaining banking information prior to planning robberies.

He has a penetrating stare, like he can read your mind when he looks at you.

He is a former member of the "BANDITOS" gang, where he picked up the nickname "BOSTON".

He loves young, beautiful women, and he spends money lavishly on them to take them to bed.

He can look at you and smile as he plans to kill you. Has good "poker" face.

He is the consummate "professional," especially in robbing banks.

He has a deep baritone voice, well modulated and sexy to entice women.

He loves to throw poker games with "multi-million" dollar pots, lasting for days at a time, where he provides the players with plenty of excellent food, all the drugs they want, personal bodyguard protection for each, women for sexual favors, etc.

He is a "cold-blooded" professional killer!

# "ADRIAN"

(COVER)            Auto parts retailer and auto repair.
(NICKNAME)         "El rastrero"
(GANG Position)    Meticulously plans out bank and jewelry robberies.
(Description)       5'5" tall, 165-170 lbs., curly hair, black eyes, dark
                   complexion
(Criminal Record)  None

### (Background Information)

Is highly intelligent, is fabric designer for COLTAGER Co., which designs fabrics for other companies.

He is well disciplined, and has a wife of exquisite beauty, along with two children, whom he loves very much.

He favors Cadillacs, and Subaru cars, loves to hoard gold, and is very, very ambitious

He is the "planner" of crimes that go like clockwork, and can plan a crime down to the last fine detail, literally designing a "blueprint" to successfully pull it off.

He will rob you behind your back, and he knows many crooked police officers

He loves to drink expensive wines and liquors. He loves tall women, especially ones taller than he is.

He goes to another state to cheat on his wife, so that she will not find out about it.

He stole $11,000,000,00 from another gang he was doing business with, and was killed for doing it when they found out it was him.

He is a "cold blooded" killer that will carry out a "hit" against you, especially when money is involved.

# "GERMAN"

(COVER)          Family Business – Fruit Distributor
(NICKNAME)      "EL NAVAJA"
(GANG Position)   Motorcycle rider for getaways from bank robberies,
                     and for leaving scene of "contract" killing
(Description)     6'1", 185 lbs., lean build, white complexion
(Criminal Record)  NONE

## (Background Information)

He is a regular "family guy", and has a wife and children that he loves very much.

He loves to ride motorcycles, especially "Yamaha".

He is a "loner".

He works sometimes in the family business, which is at a fruit distribution warehouse.

He presents himself as a gentle, almost "timid" man, but is a "cold-blooded" killer when it involves money or business. He is quite lethal, believing his outward behavior.

He loves dogs, doesn't drink alcohol, does not use cocaine, and he loves beautiful women for sexual pleasure.

He also loves expensive foods & wines, and "TANGO" music. Women love him, as he spends a lot of money on them.

He is very loyal to his friends.

As far as his "criminality," he is very inconspicuous.

When it comes to killing someone, all he wants to know is who, when, how, where, and how much he will be paid to do it.

# "JUAN PABLO"

| | |
|---|---|
| (COVER) | Auto parts retailer and auto repair. |
| (NICKNAME) | "EL-LOCO" ("CRAZY MAN") |
| (GANG Position) | Security |
| (Description) | 6'2", 180 lbs., brown eyes & hair, white complexion |
| (Criminal Record) | Arrested three times previously for bank robbery but was never convicted of them. |

(Background Information)

As a child, he dreamed of becoming a "highly-trained surgeon. He was abandoned by his father at an early age. He took to the streets after moving in with his grandmother, and was influenced into the criminal life by street people, prostitutes and other criminals. He made many bad decisions at a young age, especially to disregard all of the moral principles he had been taught by his parents. After prostitute introduced him into sexual pleasures, he came to equate sex as "love", and frequented brothels continuously, instead of marrying and raising a family.

He loves women, especially young, beautiful blonds.

He loves automatic weaponry, especially UZI'S (in 9 mm) machine pistols.

Joined the Colombian Army to become an "expert" in all weapons.

He sees bank robberies as payback to a corrupt government, because of what he went through as a child.

He thinks like "Robin Hood", which is to take from the rich people and give to the poor.

Sees "Colombian" government as a bunch of corrupt politicians that take money and civil rights away from the poor population.

He is a lonely person, and a "loner" that doesn't hang around with a lot of people.

Most of his time is spent alone.

He is very insecure, and has many personal doubts

He tries to make people believe that everything is ok, when it is not.

He wants to prove himself to other members of the gang that he has joined.

He has lost all faith in humanity, and believes that there is no hope for him.

He doesn't care if he lives or dies.

He is the first to volunteer for a crime, as he wants to be killed by the police or other criminals, as he doesn't have the courage to take his own life.

He uses a lot of drugs and alcohol.

He is an incessant "womanizer".

He loves good Italian food, and Italian clothes especially suits made of silk or "shark"-skins.

He is very generous with his friends.

He loves good movies, especially "tear-jerkers" and comedy.

He loves to own "finely-built houses.

He loves fine, expensive cars, especially "B.M.W.'s"

He loves fine works of art, and artists.

He loves to cook "gourmet" foods.

He loves to practice contact sports, soccer, and football.

He is a very "passive" person.

He becomes another person when called upon to kill someone for the "Cartel".

He sometimes that his "heart" is made of stone, because he had no bad feelings about killing the enemies of the "Medellin" Cartel, as other criminals.

He pays for "love," (sex"; because he doesn't believe in real "love").

He became the judge, jury and executioner of bad people because he sees a lot of corruption in life.

He loves his family very much.

He believes women should be treated right, and will be quick to kill you if he sees you mistreat a woman, child, or elderly person.

He is loyal and faithful to friends.

He is very faithful in keeping secrets.

He loves money, and what it can buy him.

Likes to stay home as much, as he can, watching good movies and using cocaine.

－－－－－－－－－－－－－－－－－－

He will die for his little sister who has always been there for him, like a shadow. She been with him throughout his journey through the criminal underworld, and can bear witness to his past, and his conversion.

She was the first to see how "God" had changed him, and was amazed at his transformation into a Christian "man of God."

After seeing what God did to "Juan Pablo", she became a "Christian" herself!

# "ALEX"

(COVER)           Auto parts retailer and auto repair.
(Nickname)        Burbuja
(GANG Position)   THE "BOSS"!
(Description) —    6' tall, 190 lbs. brown eyes, dyed black hair, olive complexion

Looks like the American actor "Lee Van Cleef", and acts like him too.

## (BACKGROUND INFORMATION)

Likes fancy Italian clothes.

Owns an expensive house with Italian marble used throughout.

Uses porcelain dishes and utensils.

Has "mountains" of money put away from bank robberies and cocaine smuggling.

He is a big womanizer that loves to date and spend lots of money on women, then take them to bed for sex.

He has a "beautiful" wife and 2 children.

His favorite hobby is collecting fancy classic cars, mainly 1930's replicas of FORD coups and roadsters.

He also collects classic "Cadillacs".

Loves guns, and uses silencers all of the time to kill with, so as not to alert others.

He is a very heavy user of drugs and alcohol.

He likes to gamble, especially "high-stakes" poker games.

He has lots of bodyguards to protect him from his many enemies.

Most people fear him as a dangerous man.

He is very well connected with the heads of the "Medellin" Drug Cartel.

He is known as an excellent bank robbery planner

In the early 1980's, he stopped robbing banks, and became involved in narco-trafficking, primarily cocaine.

If you violate his rules, he will hunt you down and kill you.

He gained the nickname "Burbuja" in the 1980's because, if you don't do what he says, he will have you killed.

He always has many beautiful women, and when he is finished with them, he'll let you have them for sexual pleasure also.

The only woman he is "jealous" of is his wife, and he'll kill you quick if he thinks you're looking at her."

He has been to prison several times, and has vowed never to be arrested again, or taken alive.

He loves exotic birds, and raises them in his backyard, which is surrounded in wire mesh, with a tree in the middle, next to his swimming pool.

Every year, on December 31st, he opens the doors and pulls back the wire mesh, and releases the bird to go free.

He is still alive, hiding in "Europe" somewhere, and probably has had plastic surgery to change his appearance.

He is wanted by the "Colombian" Authorities, as well as the criminal elements that want to kill him.

# CHAPTER 8

# "The Wind Fleet"

We were called "The Wind Fleet for good reason, by both the public and the Law Enforcement Authorities. Our "group", there are seven of us and were known to successfully pull of some of the most daring and well planned and orchestrated bank robberies ever staged in the cities and towns of Colombia.

We operated like "clock-work," coming in fast like a strong wind blowing through town from one end to the other. We were "gone" before you ever even realized we'd "arrived".

One after the other we'd rob the banks, getting done quickly and efficiently, and get clean away before any authorities could arrive to try to stop us.

From the beginning, we knew that, to be successful, we'd have to plan our robberies very meticulously in every detail, down to the last second, and never leave anything to chance. We were professionals, and it always showed in the execution of our crimes.

Most importantly for all of us, we wanted to get as much money in cash as possible from each robbery we pulled off.

So, to that end, we would cultivate a "conlas" inside the banks we intended to rob ahead of time.

Usually it would be one of the banks "executive" who would tip us off. For an equal share, give us the information as to when there was going to be a large amount of cash on hand at that particular bank branch, so that we could plan accordingly.

The "contact" at the bank would get an equal share of our take on the robbery in "exchange" for the information.

We would have been "casing" that location for several weeks prior, scoping out their security cameras locations, and other security measures that they may have in place, noting the closing times each day, patrols, etc.

We would also study the town's traffic patterns, noting the best routes to make good our getaways from the bank after the robberies.

We'd time our robberies so that the flow of traffic was fast and thin, to aid our escapes.

We'd have a "professional" photographer take a "montage" of photographs of the surrounding streets, to plan out the best roads to use to get away quickly when we left the banks.

We'd also find out in advance who the manager, and assistant manager was, as we knew that they were the ones who held the keys to the vault doors.

One of them was usually our "inside man" at that bank branch, who gave us the information of how much cash was on hand, in "millions".

We would always use two cars for every robbery we pulled.

One car would be the one that we would arrive in at the bank, so that anyone that was watching would note the make and model and color of the car, and also the license plate number.

We would have our bags for the money, and our weapons, in the first car. It would drop us off, then leave and go to our second car, where the first car would be abandoned.

They would then leave in the second car, which would go to an agreed upon location to wait for us.

As we would exit the bank after the robbery, we would be picked up by the riders on motorcycles, where we would jump on the back, and all of the bikers would leave the bank, going different directions

Blacks away, the motorcycle riders would drop us off, and we would take taxis, or buses, and meet at our agreed upon location where we would count the money, divide it up, and watch T.V. & listen to the radio news, to hear what the police were doing in trying to find us.

Our second car would be burned to destroy fingerprints or other evidence in it, and we would enjoy the money and plan our next bank job. Our leader's name was "Gamusa", which, when translated into "English", means "Swede", (and is pronounced "Swāde".).

He was 49 years old, and had the most experience of any of us in our line of work, so to speak. He was a brilliant man with lots of great ideas on how to accomplish our objectives. His word was gold, and he was very trustworthy and reliable.

One day, when we met to plan our next bank robbery, "Swede" brought along a friend of his, named "Marcos", whom he told us was very courageous. He was a professional photographer, and was also an experienced bank robber.

"Marcos" explained that he was looking for a place to stay with his family, and asked if we knew of a place he could rent.

One of our associates, named "Manuel", that helped us out occasionally when we needed to do a big job, had an apartment that was located on the second floor of his house, that he said he'd rent to Marcos and his family.

Several weeks later, after Marcos rented the apartment, he came home to find Manuel dead on the floor.

Marcos, not wanting Manuel's body to be found in his apartment, rolled the body, up in a large rug, and put it in his car, taking it out to the country to dispose of it. he then covered it with lots of gasoline and set it on fire, burn it to destroy the body completely, and burying the charred remains.

A "gopher" for us named "Jonathan", came to us and told us that Marcos had killed "Manuel and had burned his body out in the woods.

I was so angry when I heard about this that I vowed to kill "Marcos" and his entire family to avenge Manuel's death. I swore that I would kill him on site.

Jonathan then went back and told Marcos that I was infuriated, and had vowed to kill him and his family!

Marcos then disappeared, taking his family with him.

"Swede" then received a phone call from Marcos, who told him what had actually happened, and it turned out that Manuel had been killed by some of his enemies. Marcos had not killed him after all, as he had had no reason to.

Swede then went to where Marcos was hiding, and brought him to us. When Marcos arrived, he and I started looking at each other very hard, determined to try to figure each other out.

For about a year after that we continued to work together robbing banks, and for some reason he wanted me to be around him all of the time.

I thought that maybe he was trying to be friendly, but then realized that he wanted to know where I was at all times.

Shortly after that," out of the blue", he told me that his wife was pregnant, and asked me if I would be the child's "Godfather"!

I was "taken aback" at first, trying to figure out why it was me he was asking this of.

I then remembered an old saying from my ancestors, which was:

"Keep your friends close to you, but keep your enemies closer".

So I never trusted him very much.

Then, I found out later that, in reality, Marcos was a vicious, "cold blooded" killer, when he "machine-gunned" Carlos, along with a good "friend" of his, "Diego" the photographer, that he'd known for years, in cold blood, like it meant nothing to him to do so. I had went to Diego, laying on the road, bleeding to death, and ended his painful suffering. I then realized that if he could "machine-gun a "good friend" that easy, then what would keep him from killing me and my family, especially after he'd heard earlier that I had planned to kill him on sight.

I never took my eyes off of him, or trusted him very much, after he'd shot his good friend, Diego.

He was a "stone-cold" killer who had absolutely no remorse whatsoever for killing anyone, even his close friends.

# CHAPTER 9

························································

## February 14TH
## 1980

# "The Call"

To the outside world, we were just like everyone else in the neighborhood, with a house, a wife and kids, a car or two, and an ordinary life to live. But our lives were far from "ordinary" in many ways.

Today, after having been contacted by "Swede", our leader, we all knew the routine. We were to meet at the shop behind our auto parts business that we used as a "cover" for our criminal activities.

One by one we arrived by different methods of transportation. Some of us come by "bus", some arrived in a "taxi", some walked in, and one rode a bicycle which wearing a pair of shorts and a "tank-top" T. shirt those said "WHO? ME"! printed in capital letters across the front. That was "Jonathan", our "Pimpollo"! He's the "clown" of our group, unfortunately.

Once everyone is present, we get comfortable, making cups of coffee, lighting our cigars, making thick sandwiches of meat and cheese, and a few making a "mid-day" cocktail of bourbon, or rum and soda. After enjoying some small talk, it's time to get down to some serious business.

Our group leader, "Swede", addresses us, and gets our attention:

"Swede" – "25,000,000 "Pesos'" gentleman! That is in "million"!" he says to a room that gets very quiet, very fast!

"As all of you know, "Artudo" has always given us good useful information", he says to everyone. Artudo, or "Arty", as he is sometimes referred to, is a very rich man who is fast of the "high society" crowd. He is very well educated, and is in charge of the entire banking community in Medellin, Colombia.

At 6'2" and 275 lbs. he is a big man, with an imposing physical presence. His suit is very immaculate and well tailored, made of silk in midnight blue, as is his shirt and dress tie. His shoes are hand-made "Italian", and very expensive. He wears at least three gold and diamond rings on each hand. Even though he has a large fat belly, and a large butt, his clothing and manner of speaking to you exudes wealth and sophistication. He is very well connected politically and socially. He is mostly bald on top, with brown hair on the sides.

Being in charge of the banking community in Medellin, a city of approximately 1.5 million people he knows which banks will have how much cash on hand on any given day, especially after the holidays.

Being connected to high finance and high society, he also knows where they store and cut jewels, especially diamonds, emeralds and rubies.

He is the "Eagle-Eye", who tells Swede where and when they will be cutting the stones and how many jewels, and how much cash they will find at that location.

"Artudo" is invaluable to us for information and always gets a full share of the take from our efforts, based on the information he provides us.

Swede – "We've been casing the bank's location for over six weeks now, and Artudo says they will have at least $25 million pesos on the day after "Valentine's Day". "We hit them tomorrow"!

"Jonathan", are the cars ready for us"?

Jonathan - "Got.–'em ready to go, "Boston". I got–'em from Venezuela, so they can't be traced too easily." "The license plates are current, but are from other cars".

Swede – "Good job, "Pimpollo"! says Swede!

Swede – "Marcos, do you have the photos of the streets and surrounding area of the bank?"

Marcos – "Yes, right here, "Boston". "I have the exit route all planned out for the thinnest traffic and quickest way out of the area after we hit them".

Swede – "Great", good job! How about the security guards, and the opening times of the bank"?

Juan Pablo – "I've got that down pat, Boston". "They have two security officers that will be stationed out in front of the bank when it opens up at seven am. You have four security cameras at this location "Boston". One at the front entrance, one at the rear entrance, one covering the teller's cages, and one in the vault area. The guards leave after the doors open for business and go on break, and there are two of them, armed with .38 caliber pistols".

Swede — "Thanks, Loco"!

As you know, guys, we're going to hit them fast and get out quick, especially since this one is in broad daylight! So I don't want any screw ups or second guessing on anything. I want it to go like "clock-work," as we'll have approximately eight minutes to get it done and get gone before the security patrol comes back around. Am I understood by everyone"?

Everyone nods and says "yes" in unison.

Swede – "Adrian, do you have the addresses of the bank's manager and assistant manager?"

Adrian – "Yes, Boston, I have it right here, and I've driven past their houses several times. Also, they usually arrive at the bank at about six A.M., and each of them separately carries one vault key. We'll need both keys to enter the vault." "They also, have the combinations to the vault we'll need."

Swede (Boston) – "Thanks Adrian, I like your attention to detail."

"El navaja", have you got the motorcycles and riders ready?"

German (El navaja) – "Sure do, "Boston", I'll have the bikes and riders waiting about a block away, ready to come when they get the word from us".

Swede (Boston) – "Great"!

"Marcos, what about the briefcases and weapons for El-Loco and El navaja?"

"Do you have them ready?"

Marcos – "Sure do, Swede. I modified the interior of the briefcases to hold the "UZI's" so that they can't be seen. I used the 9 mm. weapons with the short barrels, so that they'll fit inside the cases, and I rigged the trigger so that they can be fired through a hole at the end of the briefcase if need be. All you need to do is squeeze a small lever on the briefcase's handle. I used four inch "silencers" to suppress them, and if they are used, there won't be any shell casings left behind, as they'll be "contained" in the case".

Swede – "Good work, Marcos, I like that!"

Juan Pablo – "Great, just what we need, our very own "James Bond" 0078" Juan Pablo says, "sarcastically".

Swede – "Juan Pablo, an the army uniforms ready"?

Juan Pablo – "They're right here, Swede. Yours is for a Lt. Colonel, and the others are enlisted rank". "I have the boots, too!"

Swede – "Good work, Juan Pablo. You're in charge of security out in front of the bank. Take "El navaja" with you, and dress as businessmen in three-piece suits. Don't shoot unless absolutely necessary".

Juan Pablo – "Gotcha, Boston"!

Swede – "Ok, Guys, we'll meet back here at three A.M. tomorrow morning. don't go out partying tonight, as I need everyone alert and sober till we're finished with this. Am I understood"?

Everyone – "You Got it, Swede"!

Swede – "Alright, get some rest this evening"!

   After having arrived separately at their planning location, "Swede" addresses the gang members.

Swede – "OK, let's go over it one more time, guys"!

   "Jonathan, make sure the cars are warmed up and ready for when I call you on the two-way radio. I'll need you there immediately, like 30-45 seconds ok"!

Jonathan – "Got it, Swede"!

Swede – "Marcos, Adrian, get dressed in the army uniforms now, with the boots polished!"

(Both answer up)— "Got it done"!

"El navaja" – "Bikes & bikers are ready, Boston"!

Swede – "Good show, German"!

"Juan Pablo; you'll have the front with German"!

Juan Pablo – "Dressed and waiting, Swede"!

Swede – "Good"! "Now let's get going. It's 3:35 am and we need to be at the bank managers house by 4:00 am!"

"Marcos and Adrian, you two come with me, now".

"Swede", now dressed as a "Lt. Colonel" in formal military dress uniform, exits the rear of the shop, and, along with Adrian and Marcos enters the military jeep that they had obtained from a "military surplus" sale. Marcos and Adrian are dressed in "camouflage" fatigues, as "enlisted" men.

"Swede sits up front in the passenger seat as Adrian drives, while Marcos sits in back.

Pulling up in front of the bank manager's house in an "upper-middle-class" neighborhood in "Medellin", they park in front of the house, exit the jeep, and approach the dwelling.

As they get to the front door, Marcos knocks loudly on the door and waits several moments before it is opened by a balding, "middle aged" man of about 50 years of age.

Bank Manager – "May I help you"? he says to the three "military men" standing in front of him.

"Swede" – "Sir, may we step inside for a moment?"

Bank Manager – "Of course, Colonel", he says, as he steps aside, allowing the three men to enter the house.

"Swede" – "Sir, military intelligence has obtained information that there is going to be an attack on the mall by a "terrorist" organization, and that an employee in your bank is helping to financially support that organization. We need your help, sir, to get to the bank early, and to be inside, and out of sight, before any of the employees arrive for work, so as not to tip him, or any of his "terrorist friends" before we can take him into custody and interrogate him. It is very important that we have your full cooperation, sir"!

Bank Manager — "Of course, Colonel, whatever you need, just ask."

"Swede" — "Thank you, sir, and I apologize for interrupting your schedule at this early hour of the morning".

Bank Manager – "That's quite alright, Colonel, I was up already anyway".

   "What time do we need to be there, Colonel?"

"Swede" – "At approximately 05:30 am, sir"!

   "It's 04:45 now, sir, we'll leave in fifteen minutes. We'll take you with us in the jeep"!

Bank Manager – "Fine, that will allow me to finish my breakfast before we leave".

"Swede" – "Sorry again for the early interruption, sir".

0530 AM

   As Swede, Adrian, Marcos and the bank's manager arrive, they all get out except "Adrian," who has been told by Swede to put the jeep where it can't be seen.

Juan Pablo and "El navaja" (German), dressed in business suits, are not sitting across the street at the "cafeteria", eating a sandwich and watching the front of the bank.

"Jonathan" is two blacks away, awaiting word to bring "getaway" car number one to the bank.

0600 HRS. – The bank employees begin to arrive at the bank, and are told to go to the large office in back of the bank as they come in through the door.

The bank's security is in front of the bank, as they are supposed to be.

0640 HRS. — The bank manager and assistant manager are then told that this is actually a bank "robbery" and to do what they are told, so that nobody will get hurt!

"Swede" – "Ok, you know the drill! Bring me the keys to the "vault", now!" He says to both the manager and assistant manager, as all three men train their automatic military assault rifles on them.

Bank Manager — "Ok, yes, we have the keys to the vault, but please don't shoot anyone"!

"Swede" – "Both of you, use your combinations and keys, and get that vault door open, now"!

Bank Manager — "Of course, yes"! he says, as he tells the assistant manager to insert his key into the vault door. Then, using their separate combinations, they open the vault door and step inside.

"Swede" — "Good, now the both of you lay down on the floor, "face-down", and don't move"!

Both Managers – "Yes, sir"!

"Swede" – "Put the cash in the bags, "quickly", he says to "Marcos", as Adrian keeps the banks employees covered in the large back office.

Marcos pulls out the money bags and begin filling them up with stocks and stocks of cash

Within 10 minutes he has emptied the vault of its money supply, leaving only a few small bills and some coins on the shelves.

Swede and Adrian then "hog-tie" the manager and assistant manager, and leave them on the floor of the empty vault.

0650 HRS. Swede calls "Jonathan" on the two-way, telling him to "stand-by"!

At this time, Juan Pablo and "El navaja" hear Swede's voice call Jonathan to "stand-by", and they casually walk across the street from the cafeteria to the front of the bank and stand there as if they are waiting for a "taxi" to pick them up.

They are watching the patrol car, waiting for it to leave.

0655 HRS. — The patrol car leaves from the front of the bank.

0656 HRS— Swede calls "Jonathan" on the "walkie-talkie" again, saying "Go, Go, Go"!

At the same time, the motorcycle riders also hear "Go, Go, Go" over their radio, which is their signal to start up and wait for the getaway car to pass them, by where they're parked about a block away from the bank.

0657 HRS– Swede and Marcos and Adrian exit the bank carrying the money bags just as "Jonathan" pulls up in front of the bank. Swede is "covering" the office door, preventing employees from leaving.

0658 HRS — "Swede" – "Fast, let's move, everything into the car"! he says, as all three of them throw the money bags and their weapons into the car!

"Jonathan" then quickly leaves the bank, heading for their agreed upon meeting location, where he has a second car waiting. He puts the money from the first car into the second, then leaves after wiping it down. As "Jonathan" leaves, the three turn towards "Juan Pablo and El navaja", who have thrown their briefcases into the car also, and says "Let's go", as the five motorcycles arrive in front to pick them up, taking them in five different directions.

0659 HRS Approximately a mile away, in different location the motorcycle riders drop of the men, who take the "bus", a "taxi", and "walk" back to the planning location, located at the "auto parts shop".

As the men arrive back at the shop by different methods, from different directions, they find "Jonathan" already at the shop, waiting for them.

"Swede" — "Fantastic job, guys"! he says to everyone in the shop, as he pulls down the money bags and begins counting the stack of bills out the table in eight piles.

Six equal shares will go to them, one will be given to "Artudo" for the information he had provided them, and a share for the "bikers" to split among themselves.

"Swede" — "Ok, guys, we got $15,000,220 pesos for the haul, which, spit 8 ways is approximately $1,900,000 pesos each"!

"Not bad for a morning's work, gentleman"!

"Don't spend it all in the same place, ok", he says, as he calls a taxi to come pick him up out front.

"Jonathan" starts whistling as he puts his share into his "back-pack", after counting it three times

He puts the "back-pack" on over his "tank-top" T-shirt that says "WHO? ME"!, and gets on his bicycle as he puts his "baseball" cap on backwards, he sat "wiggling" his butt from side to side, and, in a "high-pitched" sing-song voice, starts repeating over and over again, as he rides away on his bicycle:

"Jonathan" = "LIVING LA-VIDA LOCA"!

"LIVING LA-VIDA LOCA"!

The guys just turn and look at each other, shake their heads, and say:

"Where did we get this guy?" and "bust out laughing"!

## March
## 1980

After hitting the bank for fifteen million in cash, splitting the money, and laughing all the way home, we started planning our next robbery.

Things were going great in "Medellin", as we had all the money we needed to enjoy the "good life".

Our business, the Auto Parts Store and repair shop, was busy making money for us, but it was also "laundering" money from our bank robberies.

After getting my "cut" from the heist, I purchased a "1957" Cadillac convertible that was in "mint" condition, as I love "classic" cars. I also bought a new 1980 BMW "Roadster", and a 1980 Harley Davidson "Superglide" 1200 motorcycle, fully dressed with "fairing" and saddlebags.

I found a "great" deal on a house just outside of "Medellin", with five bedrooms, five bathrooms, a swimming pool, and a four car garage. It was a "steal" at only 450,000 pesos. I already had four other houses in "Medellin", but I loved the "Italian" styled architecture, as I love all things "Italian".

A short time afternoon "Valentine's Day" bank job, "Swede" received another call from our friend, "Artudo".

He told "Swede" that he had another job for us lined up, and Swede agreed to meet with him and discuss it.

After being filled in on the details, "Swede" came back and told us that "Arty" had lined up a jewelry, cash, porcelain and clothing robbery for us, of about $250,000,000 pesos in value.

It was at a warehouse when they cut diamonds, emeralds, rubies, sapphires and other "precious" stones for sale to retail outlets. They also had "priceless" porcelain and china sets, jade and expensive clothing stored there in their "vault", along with a large amount of cash on hand.

We quickly and unanimously agreed on doing the heist, and began planning the robbery, putting together everything we'd need to do the job.

We went to "Bogota", Colombia; and rented a house there for us to stay in. "Jonathan" drove our truck to "Bogota" from "Medellin", as it had a custom made "double-floor" hidden in the bed that we used to transport our machine guns and automatic pistols, since these items could not travel with us aboard any commercial aircraft.

We also brought women with us, to make it look like we were just another "regular" family that was moving into the "middle-class" neighborhood.

We put the warehouse under surveillance, and within thirty days we had our robbery planned out meticulously, down to the very last minute detail.

One part of the plan involved a very beautiful female shoplifter named "Theressa", that Adrian found for us.

He disguised her in a "French" maid's type uniform, and we had her repeatedly pass by a guard at the warehouse every day for about three weeks, until he became infatuated with her. She was wearing the black and white skirt and blouse, where the skirt barely covered her "butt," and the blouse barely held her ample cleavage back from tumbling out in front.

After three weeks of seeing her walk down the street with her little dog on a leash, he finally took the "bait," and on a Friday evening, he asked her how she was doing and where she worked.

She told him, as was our plan, that she worked for a lady there in "Bogotá". He then invited her to come spend some time with him the next night, a "Saturday".

She agreed, and said that she would bring them something to eat also.

The next evening she shopped at a cafeteria and picked up some pastries and yogurt.

Adrian was waiting, and he had a syringe full of a "knock-out" drug to put the guard to sleep.

Using the long needle, he injected the drug into the container of yogurt without ever opening it.

"Theressa" then took the food to the warehouse and gives it to the guard, who eats it hungrily.

We were waiting around the corner, and we heard her scream very "loudly"! We ran to the warehouse, and the guard was holding on to "Theressa" around her legs.

He was crawling on the floor and saying "this prostitute drugged me"!

We then realized that we hadn't used enough of the drug that was put into the yogurt.

We tied him up and gagged him, grabbing his keys to the warehouse doors.

A friend of ours, "Josh", was an expert "safe-cracker", and Swede called him, telling him that we needed him, "pronto!"

While we waited for "Josh" to arrive, we started loading up our car with "expensive" clothes, ceramics, porcelain, etc. and had packed it full 8 or 10 times as it left and returned again and again.

At eleven thirty pm. "Josh" finally arrives at the warehouse. He is 54 years old, 5'4", brown eyes and hair, white complexion, and wears thick glasses. He weighs 215 lbs. and is "fat"! He is beginning to "bold" in the back, and is wearing a black "Italian" suit.

At approximately 1:00 AM in the morning "Sunday", he gets the vault open for us!

"We took everything"!

At six thirty AM. "sharp" on Sunday morning, we've completely cleaned out the warehouse of all of the ceramics, porcelains, Jade, diamonds, emeralds, rubies, sapphires, fur coats, silks, and all of the cash from the vault! Absolutely nothing is left!

Our total take is "astounding"!

Back at the house, the "buyers" we had contacted started arriving to look over the valuables, making offers to purchase them from us.

We ended up "netting" $11,000.000.00 dollars

We had picked out some really nice, big "expensive" pieces of jewelry out of the large leather bag for the women we had with us. They were very "happy" about that.

"Jonathan" then took the bag to sell the jewelry and diamonds for us, and promptly disappeared. We went back to "Medellin" after the heist, and started planning more robberies.

About seven months later a friend of ours told us that they had found "Jonathan, and that he was living in an "upscale", wealthy neighborhood in "Bogota"

We flew back to Bogotá, and we found the house where he was living at. After watching his residence for several days, we picked a Sunday to confront him

As we approached the house, we found the "house keeper" out in front of the garage door, sweeping. I got her by the arm, and told her "this is not about you", and told her to tell me where to find "Jonathan" at, and to stay in the garage till we left.

I locked the front door and back door after we came in the back. "Jonathan" was still sleeping with his wife in their bedroom.

All of us surrounded the bed in the "master" – bedroom, and "Swede" pulled out his .45 caliber automatic and hit the side of the large oakwood bed several times, "hard"!

"Jonathan" woke up with a startled look on his face, which became a look of "terror" when he saw our guns pointed at him!

"What did you do with our "jewels"? Swede asked him, pointing his .45 at Jonathan head!

"Don't kill me, please don't kill me", begged Jonathan as he pleaded for his life after hearing Swede cock his hammer on the .45 automatic!

"I have your stuff, and I can get it for you if you'll let me make a phone call", he said, as he shook violently beneath the covers on his "king"-sized bed!

"One call, no games"! said "Swede", as he kept his .45 pointed at Jame's temple.

Jonathan then picked up the phone and punched some numbers, waited a moment, then began talking to someone on the other end of the line.

After a few moments of conversation," Jonathan handed the phone to "Swede", saying "he wants to talk to you"!

"Swede"– "Yeah, who is this"?

"Alphonso"– "Hey Swede, it's me, Alphonso"!

"Swede"– "Al?, what the…"?! "What's going on here"?

"Alphonso"– "Swede, don't kill Jonathan"! "I have your money here, in my safe"! Come on back here to "Medellin" and I'll give it to you. You have my word on it. I'll be expecting you".

"Swede"– "That's good enough for me, "Al"! We'll be there before midnight. We won't kill him"! (The call ends).

"Swede" "Let's go guys"! Swede says to us, as he puts his .45 auto back into his waistband!

"Swede"– "I know this man, guys, and he says he has our money. His word is "gold", and always has been! He is "very" well connected, and very "powerful". "We do not kill Jonathan"!

("All of us") "If you say so, "Boston", that's good enough for us", we agree in unison, as we put away our weapons and leave "Jonathan" and his wife sitting up on their bed, totally "terrified"!

Jonathan is sitting up on his bed, trembling violently and as white as "aghast", while his wife is sitting next to him, almost catatonic, and "mummified" with fear!

We flew back to "Medellin" that afternoon, arriving just before dark.

We all decided that we would go see Alphonso the next day, and were exhausted from travelling anyway.

We weren't worried about our "jewels", or the money for them now, as "Swede" had told us that Alphonso's word was "gold", and that he was a very "powerful" man in Colombia. "Swede" said he would bet his "life" on Alphonso's "word of honor", and that was good enough for us. "Swede" was a professional bank robber from way back, and had known Alphonso from those times in his past.

The next morning we drove to a village outside of Medellin, named "Aquacatala", where Alphonso lived. The village was full of "expensive" houses, and even bigger "mansions". It was located at the fact of a mountain, on top of which "Pedro Diaz" had built his own personal fortress in "Embigado", which translates to "the Woods".

When we rang the doorbell, a very "beautiful" woman answered the door.

"Swede"– "We're here to see Alphonso, "ma'am"!

"Woman"– "Please come in gentleman, Alphonso's been expecting you. I'll tell him you're here. Please sit down, and make yourselves comfortable.

It was there that we started to notice the very expensive and extravagant furnishings inside Alphonso's house.

He had "priceless" paintings by Monet, Degas Renoir, and Picasso, and several very expensive porcelain figurines in plain view.

We just looked at each other and whistled softly at all of the "opulence" in front of us, and tried to calculate in our minds how much money it must have cost for all of it!

Several minutes later "Alphonso" walked into the living room with a large cardboard box and dumped a very large pile of money onto the top of a big coffee table, spilling a lot of it onto the floor as it overflowed the table.

"Alphonso" – "Do you agree with this amount, gentleman?

As we looked at the "huge" pile of cash in front of us, we tried to calculate how much was there!

We then noticed that it was in "U.S." dollars, and that all of the stacks of bills we in hundred dollar bills! There was almost five million dollars sitting in front of us!

I had never seen one man have so much money in his house before, in cash! I just kept staring at the money until "Swede" broke the silence.

"Swede" – "I believe I can speak for the rest of the group here when I say we agree".

"Alphonso" – "Good, good! I'm glad to have that taken care of, and I have a proposition for you". I have heard much about you from your associate, "Jonathan", and I have been following your exploits in the papers, and on the radio and television newscasts". I've known "Boston" for many years now, and his a good friend. "You have quite a "team" put together here and I'd like to offer you a job working for me".

"Alphonso" – "As you may already realize, your group has gained "legendary" status in the criminal world, as your robberies are always done very quickly, and successfully. You are called "The Wind Fleet" by me, and my associates".

"But, gentleman, as everyone knows, "luck" only lasts so long, and there will come a day when you are arrested, wounded, or killed on a bank job. I have seen it happen many times.

"I would like for all of you to come work for me as my "personal" bodyguards".

"I will pay each of you $100,000.00 dollars American each month."

"I will also provide you with houses to live in, machine-guns and pistols, ammo, and even the women you sleep with," and the cars you drive.

"I will pay for everything if you'll be my "bodyguards", gentleman".

"Please talk about this among yourselves, and let me know your answer in a few minutes".

We all looked at each other, and quickly decided that we'd accept his offer.

That night, Alphonso threw us a "giant" and very expensive "welcome" party to celebrate our joining his "organization" there in Medellin"!

I had absolutely no idea of what I was getting into that day, for if I had known what was in store for me, I wouldn't have just said "no" to Alphonso's offer of employment as his "bodyguard", and walked away, I would have "ran" as fast as I could.

Within six months of our accepting his offer to become his "bodyguards", Alphonso had ordered us to kill someone.

A man named "Carlos" in New York City had worked for the "Cartel" that we now were a part of, and had been a trusted associate.

He had stolen thirty kilos of cocaine that belonged to the "Cartel", and Alphonso's boss wanted him found, and "executed", as an example to anyone else that may be thinking of doing something similar. The cocaine's value was two million dollars.

Alphonso's boss, who was now "our" boss, was a man named "Pedro Diaz", who was the leader of "The Medellin Cartel", one of the most powerful cocaine suppliers in the world!

"Carlos" was found fairly quickly, as he was stupid enough to relocate to our own backyard, "Medellin", Colombia!

"Marcos" and I were assigned to do the "hi and as I watched, Marcos "machine-gunned" both "Carlos", and one of Marcos' own friends, a photographer named "Diego", that he'd been friends with for many years.

Up until this time, I had only heard rumors of how violent "Marcos" was, but I had never dreamed that he was a "cold blooded killer"!

I didn't know what I was joining when I accepted the job offer from "Alphonso", and I found myself going from bank robber to killer.

I was 23 years old, the youngest of our "gang", and had literally jumped out of the proverbial frying pan, and landed in the fires of Hell!

I had had no real idea of just what the "Medellin Cartel" was, or of how big and powerful they were, or of how "violent and dangerous" it was going to become working for them.

We stopped robbing banks altogether after we started working for Alphonso's organization and our jobs were mainly in protecting him wherever he went, collecting money, and, when the order came, "executing" our enemies.

One day "Swede" came and told us that the "boss" was moving to Miami, and wanted to know if we were coming with him. All of the others in the group agreed on the move, but I was hesitant, as things were going great in "Medellin" at the time, and we were making lots of money. I didn't really want to leave Colombia at all at that time.

Although I was against moving to "Miami" at first, I started thinking back about my "dreams" and goals that I'd had as a child.

I started remembering all of the American movies and videos that I had watched on television, and at the theaters in town, and of all the movie stars that I wanted to meet. I remembered as a child saying, "One day, I will go to the U.S."!

And then I thought "hey, I'm "twenty-three" year old already, and I need to see other places besides Colombia".

A friend I had met, "Johnny", had told me "amazing" stories about "New York City"!

Finally, I decided "Yes", why not go to Miami"!

This was the loud of "Clint Eastwood"!

I then began to look forward to "Miami", as it was a new "land", and a new "culture", and a really new "adventure" for me!

I was then very "excited", and anxious to get to the "United States Of America"!

# CHAPTER 10

# Living "La Vida Location" In Miami

After finally convincing me that moving to Miami would be owned, with lots of "beautiful girls, loads of fun, and "tons" of money, we all began to get our passports and other necessary paperwork together.

Before leaving "Colombia", we made arrangement for our properties to be taken care of in our absence. We didn't have to worry about any expenses of the move to Miami, as Alphonso told us that everything was being taken care of by the "Cartel".

We took a commercial flight from "Medellin" to "Haiti," then the "Cartel" had an associate fly us by private "Learning" jet to the "Bahamas". We stayed there a few days, then went to "Bimini" for a short vacation before taking a large, private yacht to "Miami"! And, "OH What a Yacht"!

Never before in my "life" had I ever seen a private boat as "big" as the one we took from Bimini to Miami! It was over one hundred and sixty feet long, and had a swimming pool and Jacuzzi, and a forty foot "cruiser" that could be launched from the stern at the back. It was said to cost over twenty million dollars, and took two years to build. Alphonso corrected me, as he said that it was a private ship or "Yacht", and that any boat that was fifty feet long, or more was considered a "ship". Whatever it was called, it was big and very expensive, and was like a floating "penthouse" that had everything in it! It must have cost a small "fortune" in fuel just to take it out for one day, much less to travel the "world" with it!

On our way from Bimini to Miami, there were several schools of dolphins that were swimming alongside the yacht, jumping up out of the water and cackling, as if trying to talk to us!

Just off the bow, one of them stood on its tail and began swimming backward while it looked at us as if leading us to the "promised land." It looked "spectacular"!

As we got closer to Miami, I noticed that the water was becoming clearer, and it's color even more "beautiful," like an emerald green!

The coloring of the sand on the beach was a wonderful "off-white" egg shell white that was so "pure" that it quite literally took my breath away as I had never seen anything like it before, in Colombia

I was amazed as we passed by possibly hundreds of expensive yachts, and very powerful speedboats that were pulling water skiers behind them.

There were American flags on all of the yachts showing me that I was in the most rich and powerful country in the world! It impressed me profoundly.

I felt at that moment that I had truly arrived at the "promised land"! So full of beautiful people, women in tiny bikinis, and men with lots of money and expensive cars and boats and fantastic houses on the beach. I was amazed at the wealth that I saw everywhere, and the "beauty" of the country!

Even the politeness of the people really surprised me, as everyone was so nice to you.

The streets were so clean and organized, and these were countless palm trees, and even the police cars were clean and shining.

As we drove away from the marina in a big Lincoln Town Car, I listened to some great "salsa" music on our drive to "Kendall", Florida.

When we arrived in "Kendall", I saw that it was an "upper-class", quiet neighborhood, with really nice houses and new cars everywhere packed in the driveways, and most people had swimming pools in their backyards.

"Ruben", our driver, said that hid be back that night to pick all of us up, and take us out to show as the "crazy night life" in Miami!

That night, he came to pick us up, and I was so excited and full of expectations of seeing the great things of Miami that I felt like a kid again!

He took us to a lot of different "discos", and all of them were very elaborate and expensively built.

Even the street lights were clean and beautiful to me.

I loved the "art-deco" style of the buildings, too!

When it came to picking up beautiful women I found out from "Ruben" that as long as you had cocaine and money, they were yours, "instantly"!

The last discotheque that we went to that night was one named "Studio 23", that was in "Miami Beach" on Collins and 23RD. AVE.

It had "Latin" music, and was owned by a "Colombian".

Ruben told me that "we don't come to places like this", as they are "infested" with snitches and "D.E.A." agents!

Enjoying the "nightlife" in Miami that night was like living in a "dream world"!

We had been dancing and drinking all night, and we had picked up some girls, and ended up making a "hole" on Miami Beach, and falling asleep in it.

I woke up the next morning with the sun heating up my face, like an "oven", laying next to the others, who were still sleeping.

We all woke up eventually, and went to the "Restaurant Blue Dolphin", where we ate all kinds of seafood to get our strength back.

We then went to the "Seaquarium" and saw many different kinds of sharks, then to the "Serpentarium" to see the snakes.

"Walt Disney World" was next, where we ate foods from many different countries at the "Epcot Center".

Finally, we went to "Seaworld", where we were "splashed" by our "Orca", or "killer" whale

After an entire day of "sightseeing", we returned to the house in Kendall, showered and promptly fell asleep, as it had been an "exhausting" day to say the least.

As far as our expenses there in "Kendall", all we paid for individually were our clothes, food the we ate, the booze that we consumed, and any "hookers" that we picked up for the evening.

We were provided with the cars we drove, the planes we flew, the boats, or "yachts" that we used, the drugs that we consumed, the house that we lived in, and the weapons that we needed by the "Medellin Cartel".

After several weeks in Florida "U.S.A.", I completely fell in love with this country, as I felt that it would give me everything I'd ever want in life, and much "more"!

All of us in the "Wind Fleet" rented our own large six bedroom house there in "Kendall". The house was fully furnished with everything we needed. We were cooking our own food, and doing our own shopping, and having a "terrible" time with the English language.

I cooked a seafood dish one day, and Swede was home, and I gave him a plate of it. He said that it tasted "kind of funny", and wanted to know what kind of fish I had used to make it with.

I got the can out of the trash and showed it to him, and he busted out "laughing" so hard he almost fell over off his chair onto the kitchen floor!

"Loco", he said! "You used a can of "fish" flavored "cat" food to make it with!

"No wonder it didn't taste sight," I said, as I started laughing at myself too!

The rest of the gang wouldn't let me live it down for a long time after he told them about it that night!

We were all living there in the house together, awaiting instructions from our "boss" in "Medellin" on what we'd be doing. Again, we were waiting on the "call".

Usually when we got the call, we were told to go to a certain "city", to a certain customer's "house", and that "that" person owed us "such and such" an amount of money.

We were told to collect the money by "whatever means necessary", which sometimes meant "breaking" a leg, or an arm, etc..!

Once in awhile, putting a gun to their head would suffice.

After a few months of all of us living in the same house, we finally came to the conclusion that we can't "all" continue living in the same house, as the stress and tension had built up to the point that pretty much all of us were at each other's throats, and our temper's were flairing daily!

To help relieve some of the tension, a person I had never met before brought some very beautiful women over.

They were $150.00 for the first hour, and $50.00 for each additional hour thereafter. We usually had them stay either all night, or an entire weekend.

That was the "beginning" of our stay in "Miami"

Soon, Adrian and "El navaja" went back to Colombia, saying "this place is not for me"!

"Marcos" stayed by himself then, as Swede and Jonathan got a place to share, and Alphonso and I got a place also.

As more time passed, I became much more aware of the power of the "Medellin Cartel" in Miami!

I found out that our "Cartel" had bankers on our payroll that "laundered" our drug money for us, making it look like legitimate income.

We had many "lawyers" we paid, who got cases thrown out of court on a "technicality".

We had "Judges" who overlooked criminal cases for us, "for the love of money", and lots of it!

We had "Coast Guard" commander who "looked the other way" when our cocaine shipments come in.

We had "Police Officers" that let us use their uniforms and police cars to move drugs from place to place, among other criminal purposes. A few thousand dollars is all it took!

And, basically, we were told to "beat up" the late paying customers, but not to kill them, as that way we wouldn't draw attention to the "Cartel".

We were primarily here to reinforce our existing personnel that was already established in "Miami".

To me, we, "The Medellin Cartel", were everywhere in Miami! It looked like me had "control" of Miami, the city, and all of the surrounding areas

Everywhere we went, to restaurants, bars, disco's, stores, shopping centers, strip clubs, etc. we were given the "red carpet treatment"!

That was basically our "life" in the "Cartel", "enforcing", collecting money, beatings, "strong-arm" tactics, women, lots of sex and drugs, and a lot of guns! Mostly "machine guns"!

This went on for about three years, until one day in 1983 when I decided to walk away from it all.

I started thinking about starting my own "drug" business.

But, that didn't sit very well with the rest of the "Wind Fleet," and they were determined to not allow me to walk away that easily from the "Cartel".

At the time, I was living on "Brickle" Avenue, in one of the "twin towers".

Swede called one day, and told me that he had the money I was owed, which was a very large sum, over a quarter of a million dollars.

He said they'd pick me up in about ten minutes. I told him that I'd be waiting.

When they arrived, it was raining torrentially as the skies exploded with energy!

I saw "Swede's" car as he drove down the street towards the "twin-towers", being swamped by the deluge of the downpour.

He drove down under the roof of the building to pick me up, and I jumped into the front passenger side, next to "Swede". Jonathan, the "Pimpollo", was sitting behind me in the back seat.

"Swede" pulled out of the parking lot, and just as he did I heard a "click-click" behind me.

I turned around and saw that "Jonathan" had a 9 mm "Luger", with a silencer attached, painted at my head, and that he had pulled the trigger twice without taking the "safety" off!

I quickly reached over and grabbed the gun out of his hand, while at the same time pulling my .45 caliber automatic out of its shoulder holster, pointed it at "Jonathan"', heart, and was going to kill him and "Swede", as I believed that they had planned to murder me for trying to leave the "Wind Fleet", and the "Medellin Cartel"!

As I began to squeeze the trigger of my .45, both of them burst into tears and started crying, begging me not to kill them.

"Swede" tearfully swore that he knew nothing about it, or why "Jonathan" had tried to kill me.

I thus remembered that I had had it out with "Jonathan" several months before them, over his mouth, and "back-biting", and figured that "Swede" probably didn't know anything about it!

I had never really trusted "Jonathan" anyway especially after the jewelry theft in "Bogota", and now, after this, I never would.

I looked at them for several moments right on the "edge" of blowing both of their heads right off their shoulders, and watched as they cowered in fear that they were going to be "executed" any second!

Finally, after what must have been an "eternity" to them, I released the pressure of my finger on the trigger, lowered the hammer of the .45 from its "cocked" position and opened the door behind me with my other hand, while keeping both of them covered.

"I'm going to let you live!" I told them, staring both of them down as adrenaline and anger pumped through my veins like "boiling" blood, "but if I ever see you again, anywhere, or at any time, I will not hesitate to kill you. Do you understand what I am saying?"

Both of them nodded yes, and started to breathe again as they realized they weren't going to die.

As I backed out of the passenger door, I gestured toward the street with my eyes, and said "Now go, and don't come back, or send anyone else as you know I will find you if you do!"

I watched as they quickly drove away in the downpour, my "heart" racing as I realized how close I had come to being killed.

I willed myself to calm down, and turned to walk back to my apartment, hoping that other in the area had not witnessed the incident, and contacted the police!

I came home several days later from an all night party, and entered my apartment at about 7 AM. I walked into the bedroom and sat down on the end of my bed, and for the first time in years, I began to pray, and cried out to "God"! "God", I love money, please help me find a way to love some "brain" surges as I don't want to act, or live this way anymore. "If you are real, as people say you are, please come and help me "God," please!" Amen

● ● ● ● ● ● ● ● ●

I continued to work alone for the "Cartel" though, as an "enforcer" and money collector. Then in 1984 I received a phone call from a man named "Gregorio" from New York. He was a large cocaine distributor for our "Cartel".

He told me that he had two hundred thousand dollars that was owed me, and I let him know that I was on my way to come pick it up!

That night I flew from Miami to New York, and he picked me up at "Laguardia" airport, accompanied by his wife and secretary.

His secretary's name was "Katia", and she was very "beautiful"!

As we drove towards New York City, I was totally amazed at the sheer number of really tall "skyscrapers" that we passed. I'm glad that I had my sunglasses on, as my eyes must have been as big as "silver dollars"!

Gregorio had an apartment in "Manhattan" in a very tall "high-rise" building. It was a "penthouse" suite, and was very expensively furnish as would be expected of a "multi-millionaire" cocaine distributor.

When we arrived at the "penthouse", he threw me a "welcome to New York" party with lots of booze, drugs etc.

But, I wasn't paying much attention to the partying, as I just simply couldn't take my eyes off of "Katia"! She was "delicious!"

She was actually the "beginning of the end" for me, but I had no way of knowing it yet.

At 5'4" and 125 lbs., she was "petite", a "beautiful" little bundle of "sexual" energy!

She had black "curly" hair, and smooth olive skin, and a "perfect" figure!

All of us got drunk that evening, and "Katia" was all over me, kissing me and sitting on my lap, "squirming" around like a "lap dancer" at a "Nude Bar"! "Wow", did she ever "hook" me!

That night, she and I went to a motel together, and we had the most "amazing" sexual encounters that I had ever had in my "life"! I myself had been taught by "expects", the "ladies of the evening" so to speak, and fancied myself as a "red-blooded" stud, but Katia did things to me that were "astonishing", to say the least! Just when I thought I was "all wrung out", and could not go on any longer, she would use another trick that would have me "raring to go again" like a brahma bull! Simply and utterly "ravishing"!

After over three hours of pleasure, as we laid in bed, drinks in have, and smoked a cigarette, she told me that "Gregorio" had told her that I'm the only one that can help her with a problem that she was having in "Miami"!

She then told me that a man in Miami owed her $300,000.00, and refused to pay her the money.

I agreed to help her, as with all of the "crazy" sex that we were having, I was "infatuated" to the point that I would literally do anything for her at that point.

We flew back to Miami, and went to my apartment, staying in bed for several days, making love like "wild bunnies"!

Finally, she got out of my bed, having to go to work at her business on "Flagler Avenue".

Shortly, she called me, and told me to come to her place of business at 6:30 pm that night.

After I arrived, she introduced me to her brother; "Hugo", who stood 6'3" and weighed 220 lbs. He had long, curly hair that was "black", an olive complexion, and very dark eyes!

After we introduced ourselves to one another, he laid down his plan to me, of going to the "lease" office to see the man that refused to give her back her money.

He said that "Katia" and I would pretend to be a couple that were interested in getting an apartment, and that we would then be able to see what the man looked like.

When I asked her what the problem was we needed to take care of, she explained to me that her sister, "Natalia", had bought an apartment from this guy, but when she was ready to move in, she found out that he had "switched" apartments on her.

She had then told the guy "this is not the apartment that I bought from you, and I want my money back!"

He refused to return her money to her sister

He had also "faked" her signature on the apartment sale to make it look like she had bought "that" apartment, when she had not!

Katia had then promised him that she would make him pay for what he had done to her!

We planned then to "kidnap" the man, and rented an apartment to keep him at after we grabbed him!

"Shortly", she introduced to another "brother" of hers, named "Lucas". I noticed that one of his hands was "crippled." He stood 5'3" and was "heavy-set" at 160 lbs.

"Katia" told me that "Lucas" would stay at our rented apt. and watch over the man after we "kidnapped" him, while we negotiated the ransom.

"What does this guy look like that we're going to kidnap?" I asked her.

He's about 5'8", 220 lbs., with a very "thick" beard, "pale" complexion, and very well dressed.

Several days later, we were ready to make the "grab"!

We get into the car, "Hugo" and I sit in the back seat, while "Katia" drives the car!

When we arrive at the "leasing" office, Katia and I go in together, and are approached by an old man.

"How can I help you"? he asks us.

"We'd like to look at some apartments today, as we are looking to buy!"

"Let me bring out the one you need to talk to", states the old man, as he walks to another office.

Momentarily, another man steps out of the office and walks toward us. He matches the description of the guy we're supposed to "kidnap"!

I then look out the door and made a "signal" to "Hugo", who then stepped out of the car with a "machine-gun", an UZI 9 mm with a short barrel

Hugo hid the "UZI" under his shirt until he got from the car to the bldg., while "Katia" ran back to the car, as she was planning to drive for us.

As "Hugo" came in with the "UZI", he ordered the man out the door, and told him to get into the back seat of the car.

The man did not want to go willingly! I had to punch him several times before shoving him forcibly into the back seat of the car!

Katia then "floored" the gas, and started speeding through the streets. I had to tell her twice to slow down or we'd get pulled over.

Somehow, the guy we'd grabbed ended up opening the back right hand side door, and was trying to jump out of the car.

Moving quickly, Hugo and I grab him by his clothes, wrestling with him until we finally get him pulled back into the car, which is speeding at over 60 miles an hour down the street!

When we arrived back at the rented apartment where we were going to keep him till the ransom was paid, "Katia" turned around from the front seat of the car and said after taking one look at the guy we'd grabbed, "That's not the one that we were supposed to get, that's his son"!

Although they were both of the same height, weight, and husky build, this guy was only 23 years old!

"Hugo" then said "Hold on we can hold the "son" for ransom, till the "father" pays the money"!

We agreed then that we would now have to do that, under the circumstances.

Hugo and I went out then, to a public phone that couldn't be traced back to us, and Hugo started making phone calls to this kid's "father"!

He told the father that he needs to bring $500,000.00 dollars to the "Bahamas" if he ever wants to see his son alive again!

It was $300,000.00 dollars, but now, with interest added, it was half a million!

The father then stated that he didn't have the money, and wouldn't be able to get out of the country with that amount of cash anyway!

Finally, the father asked for a few more days to get the money, and for a new "drop site" to leave it at!

We told him we'd give him a few more days to get the money together, and to put the money in two suitcases, and to bring them to a "disco" parking lot at 23$^{RD.}$ and Collins Avenue, the "Studio 23" disco!

We warned the father not to call the police, or not bring the money, as we would kill his son if he did so.

We arrived at the "Studio 23" parking lot early, at 6 PM, and called the father on a pay phone, telling him we were there.

I started looking around, and I noticed that there was a lot of movement. There was a lot of cars in the parking lot that had tinted windows, and little antennas mounted on them.

I told "Hugo" about it, letting him know that police were all over the place!

"It's a trap, the father set us up"!

"Hugo, you take off that way, and I'll go this way, otherwise they'll get us both"!

As soon as we took off running, we heard sirens and "screeching" tires as the police cars converged, with automatic weapons being chambered, and it was like a "hornets" nest that had been kicked over!

I ran towards the beach, and hid in one of the apartment buildings, in a maintenance closet!

Then, about six hours later, at 1:30-2:00 am I went back to my apartment!

The next day at about 5:00 pm, somebody knocked on my door!

When I opened the door, it was "Lucas" who said his sister, Katia, wanted to talk to me!

I went down to the parking lot to talk to her, and she said "What happened"!

"Let the man go, I'm out of it now, as the police are involved, possibly the "F.B.I". too!" I said to her!

She then said "No, I can't let him go! He saw me, and he knows who I am! You have to kill him for me!"

She pulled out some cocaine and tequila that she had in the glove box, and we both got drunk and high.

We talked about it for about an hour. I told her that there must be another way, but she kept on telling me that the kid knew who she was, and where she worked, and could identify her for kidnapping him.

I finally agreed with her, and she drove me back to the apartment where we were holding the son at.

After we arrived, I asked "Lucas" to get me a roll of tape.

When he returned with the tape, I went to the son, who had his hands tied behind his back, and I ran the tape around his head several times. The lost place I taped was his nose, and he died several minutes later!

We carried his body back to "Broward" County, and dumped it out in the "Everglades" so that no one would ever find it!

"Juan Pablo, I know that he contacted the "F.B.I"."! "Katia" said to me.

He had promised her that he would send a letter to the "F.B.I"., and tell them that he was having trouble with a family from "Colombia"!

"Juan Pablo, I've got to get out of the country!" she pleaded.

"We'll have to get to "Los Angeles", hon! I've got connections there to get the proper documents needed, passports, visa and whatever else is needed!"

We went to meet "Hugo" at the parking lot at the "Flagler Mall".

"Juan Pablo, please help my sister and brother to get out of the country. I'm leaving "tonight," myself!" "Hugo" said to me.

He then reached into his pocket and pulled out a large chunk of money, all in one hundred dollar bills!

"Here's five thousand dollars", he said to Juan Pablo"! "You'll have to drive to "L.A.", as they'll be watching the airports for you"!

Getting into the car, we left for "Los Angeles" that night, leaving the lights of "Miami" behind us.

Katia was driving her car, and we stayed at motels, and drank a lot of booze, along with using a lot of cocaine and other drugs that she had with her!

At literally every stop that we made, she wanted sex, sex, and even more sex!

I was beginning to realize that she was a true "nymphomaniac", as she just couldn't seem to get enough of it!

It took us ten days to drive to "Los Angeles", with all of the stops, we made along the way for food, lodging, fuel, and of course sex!

After we arrived in "L.A.", I went straight to my connection. Her name was "Azucena"!

"It will take some time, Juan Pablo"! she said to me.

"Let me find you a place to stay while I get this done for you", she said, and ended up finding me a place in "Hollywood".

The apartment she found for me was in the same building that "she" lived in.

Then, unknown to "Katia", I started having a sexual affair with Azucena at her apartment.

"Azucena" then introduced me to another lady that was the "manager" of the apartments! Her name was "Daniela".

Daniela opened the door for me to have an affair with her, too!

"So", I now had three different women that I was having sex with, all living in the same building, in different apartments, at the same time!

When "Daniela" found out about "Katia she wanted to know what my relationship was with her?"

I told her that Katia and Hugo were just friends, and that I was helping them.

She then started getting "jealous", and before long, all three girls were "fighting" over me!

I was going from one bed, to "another" bed, then to "another" bed, trying to keep the peace, and to "satisfy" all of them, but I was running or empty, "energy" wise, and needed a rest!

Then one day, "Daniela" was watching her television, and her "favorite" show came on!

"America's Most Wanted"!

"OH My God", she said, as she saw the faces of "Katia, Lucas and Hugo" on her "TV" screen!

They were now on the "FBI's most wanted list"

# CHAPTER 11

......................................

# "Americas Most Wanted"

After her seeing the faces of Katia and Lucas on her television screen while watching "America's Most Wanted", Daniela didn't know what to think, at first.

She thought about it for several weeks, and wondered what would happen to her relationship with "Juan Pablo" if she turned Katia and Lucas in to the authorities.

Should she confront "Katia" and her brother, and risk being hurt or killed herself?

Or should she mind her own business and keep quiet?

Did "Juan Pablo" know that the "F.B.I" was looking for Katia and her brother?

She had not heard any mention on the show of "Juan Pablo" being wanted by the authorities, and wondered if "Juan Pablo" even knew anything about what was going on.

She soon realized that it would be to her advantage to alert the "F.B.I" to the whereabouts of "Katia" and her brother, "Lucas", as that would take Katia out of the pictures, as far as she and "Juan Pablo's" relationship was concerned.

In the end, her jealousy of "Katia" made up her mind for her.

On September 14ᵗʰ, 1984 she contacted the "F.B.I." and told them that Katia and Lucas were trying to rent an apartment from her, but that she wouldn't know for sure if they were going to move in or not for a week or so.

Ten days later, on September 24ᵗʰ, 1984, she called them back, and admitted that she had lied to them initially, and told them that both "Katia", and her brother, Lucas, were already living at the apartments, and were occupying apartment # 10. Her call was made to them at approx. 9:30 pm?

They were told that if a "rust"-colored Lincoln Town Car was in # 10's parking space, that that would mean they were in the apartment.

That night, Katia and I got into an argument, and Katia left the apartment.

Lucas and I were in the apartment at the time, and I had just finished eating my dinner.

It was about 10:30 pm, and I was smoking a big "joint" to relax.

I had turned on the television in the living room, and was watching the sports report when Lucas said he saw a lot of movement in the hallway from the "shadows" under the door!

I got up and walked towards the front door, then noticed that the doorknob was turning, as someone was trying to get into our apartment!

My first thought was that it was some "hit" men sent from the "Cartel", that had somehow tracked me down in "Hollywood", California; and were going to "kill" me for leaving them!

I hurriedly pulled out my .357 magnum revolver, and stuffed a bunch of bullets into the pockets of my shorts that I was wearing at the time, and done behind the couch as the door "exploded" inward and flew off of its hinges with a loud "BOOM"!

I raised up, got into firing position, and aimed at the first person that came through the doorway. My finger began applying pressure to the trigger

I screamed "Don't move or I'll kill you"! as a man came towards me with a shotgun in his hand! My adrenaline increased, telling me to pull the trigger!

He said "Freeze, drop your weapon", but I continued screaming at him not to move any closer! My finger tightened on the trigger as I yelled at him again!

"Stop, or I'll kill you where you stand I yelled, as other people started to come into the room. My .357 aimed at his "heart," six feet away!

He then said "F.B.I." drop your weapon or I will kill "YOU"!

He then aimed the 12 gauge shotgun at my head! and said:

"F.B.I. drop your weapon"! "Lay down flat on the floor, hands behind your neck!"

"Do it NOW!"

As he screamed this at me, I heard dozens of weapons being chambered and cocked, and as I looked around me I saw more than twenty guns pointed at my head and chest, "sighting down" on me!

"Do nit NOW"! he yelled again!

Time stood still for several moments as we aimed our weapons at each other! Staring "eye to eye"!

My blood pumped through my body, quickly circulating even more adrenaline!

My finger "froze" on the trigger as the words: "F.B.I." began to have meaning in my mind, and the pressure of my finger began to subside at the realization that these were not "hit" men from the "Medellin Cocaine Cartel", they were law enforcement agents!

As we intently stared into each other's eyes, I slowly lowered my .357 magnum, got down on my knees, and laid down flat on the floor, throwing my weapons away to the side.

Again, I had come a "razor's edge" away from being killed. More agents then entered the apartment, and several went into the kitchen, where "Lucas" was still standing "paralyzed" with fear like he'd been struck by "lightning"!

I heard the agents yell at Lucas to lay down on the floor as they cuffed and arrested him. One of them then stated "We've got one in the kitchen and he's "messed" his pants!

As several of the agents began to "laugh," I yelled to "Lucas" in Spanish!

SPAN. "No diga nada"!

ENG. "Don't say anything"!

SPAN. "Dile que tu no sabe nada"!

ENG. "Tell them you don't know anything"!

SPAN. "Si tu no dice nada, ello no van a hacer nada de eso"!

ENG. "If you don't say anything, they won't know anything about it"!

Then one of the "F.B.I". agents said to me, in "Spanish":

SPAN. "Collate"!

ENG. "Be quiet"!

But, I continued to talk until I was put into the back of an "F.B.I." agent's car!

I was immediately taken to "F.B.I". Headquarters in downtown "Los Angeles", the so-called "City of Angels"!

They started interrogating me, but I denied knowing anything about any of it!

I said "I have a relationship with "Katia", and that is why she and her brother, "Lucas", are staying with me at my apartment.

They kept on questioning me all night, until about 11:00 AM the next morning.

When they stopped the interrogation, they sent me by myself to "Terminal Island Federal Institution" in San Pedro, California.

About five days after I arrived there, a lawyer came to see me.

He said "I've been appointed your lawyer, Juan Pablo, and I need to tell you that "Lucas" is telling the "Government" everything about your involvement in this case.

He then said "Juan Pablo, if you plead guilty to this case, you'll only get two years for Assault on an "F.B.I". agent with an illegal weapon" here in California.

"But if you don't plead guilty, they are going to bury you!

On July 10th, 1985 I went before Federal Judge William J. Rea in "Los Angeles".

I plead guilty to a count of an "alien in possession of a firearm", and was sentenced to two years in "Federal" prison.

The charge of "Assaulting a Federal Office was dropped in the plea bargain.

I was then extradited back to Florida to stand trial on charges against me in Miami, in Federal Court.

When I arrived, I was brought before Judge "Alcee Hastings", who set my "bond" at $4,000,000.00 million dollars!

My charges were:

1 Extortion with violent treatment
2 Extortion

I then found out that "Katia" had also been arrested, as they had her there with me at the same time, in the same courtroom.

At that moment, it hit me like a "ton of bricks" as to the "seriousness" of the crime in Florida.

She told me that she had returned to the apartment at about 1:30 AM the next morning, and that the "F.B.I". was waiting for her.

She had been arrested on the same charges as I had.

After my arraignment, I was taken to the Miami\Dade Federal Holding Center.

As soon as I arrived there, I obtained a knife, and hid it where I could get to it quickly if I needed to defend myself.

I had some drugs brought in, and since I was young and good looking, I figured that some sexual "pervert" might try to rape me, or even kill me, and I was determined to defend myself, and even kill someone if need be.

When my trial began on the "Federal" charges, I was told it would probably last about two weeks.

As the trial progressed, one day they brought in "Lucas" to testify against both his sister "Katia", and me.

When I saw him start to testify against "Katia", I exploded in a "rage" of hostile, ugly profanity at him! I said:

"Lucas, you don't know "me" personally, and I can understand you testifying against me, but what about your sister? Why are you testifying against her?"

"How in the Hell can you do this to her"?!

I stood up in the courtroom and began a profanity filled "tirade" against "Lucas", calling him every bad name I could think of!

It got to the point where it was so "out of control" that Judge "Hastings" yelled down at me from the "bench"!

"Mr. Castillo, if you don't take your seat, and "shut up," I'll have you taken out of the courtroom, and you'll watch your own trial on television, instead of being present! Do I make myself clear, sir"?

"I do not want anymore "outbursts" of any kind in this courtroom!"

— — — — — — — — — — — — — — — — — —

At the end of the trial, we were found guilty, and sentenced to 40 years in "Federal" prison on July 16TH, 1985!

Staying in "Federal" prison was not in my "life" plan at all! I had places to go and things to do!

When I was taken back to the "Holding" Center, I began making arrangements to "escape" from their custody!

I talked to one of the workers at "R & D", a place that obtained civilian clothes for prisoners that are being released from custody. He agreed to help me get civilian clothings.

I then called some of my connections on the outside, as there were several things I needed, "fast"!

"Juan Pablo" — "Juan, listen carefully! I need a fast car brought here, and left in the parking lot"!

"Put a white flag on its antenna, and leave the keys under the carpet, on the driver's side"!

"Also, put a .45 automatic on top of the left front tire, with a loaded clip in it, too"!

"Juan" – "When are you going to need this, "Loco"?"

"Juan Pablo" — "I'm going to jump the perimeter fence on Thursday night, so have it ready, ok"!

"Juan" – "No problems, "Juan Pablo"!

"Juan Pablo" – "Thanks, Juan"! "They'll have visiting hours then, and a lot more activity and confusion in the parking lot! It'll be easier to get away from here at that time"!

"Juan" – "Will do, Juan Pablo! Everything will be ready for you"!

I had everything set up, and was ready to make my way to "freedom"! I had absolutely no intention of living the rest of my "life" in prison, or of being sent to the "electric chair"!

I was psyched up, both "mentally and physically", and ready to make my move!

As I lay down in my bank on Wednesday night, I began to dream of driving away from there, and of making my way to the "Bahamas", where pretty girls, money and freedom awaited me.

Then, at about 3:00 AM on Thursday morning, I was awakened by the midnight shift officer.

"Officer" – "Castillo, get up and get dressed, and ready to go"!

"Juan Pablo" – "Get ready for what"?

"Where am I going"?

"Officer" – "You're going to court, Castillo"!

At that moment I realized that something was very "fishy", and very wrong!

I knew then that my plans were shot to Hell as far as getting away from the "Federal" Holding Center that night! It made me mad, and I felt sick inside, but I didn't have time to "cry in my soup" about it, as I had little time to get rid of escape clothes that I had hidden in my mattress before they came back to get me.

I looked out of the small window of the door to my single cell, making sure that there wasn't an officer making his rounds.

After seeing that the coast was clear, I pulled the civilian clothes out of the mattress. Then, using a razor blade that I had hidden, I began cutting the clothing into small strips of cloth, so that I could flush them down the toilet!

At 4:00 AM I had just flushed the last few strips of cloth when I heard noises in the hallway, and I knew immediately that it was me that they were coming to get. I then dropped the razor blade into the toilet bowl, and pushed the button to flush it when they opened my cell door to get me.

First, they put handcuffs on me, along with a "lock-box" over the cuffs to keep me from picking the locks of the cuffs.

Then they put a "waist-chain" around my waist, and ran a chain "through" the cuff "lock-box" and "pad-locked" the chain together tightly!

Lastly, they put "leg-irons" on my ankles, and then chained that to my waist chain with another "pad-lock"!

They wanted to make "double-sure" that I was secured, and could not escape from their custody!

As we left the "Federal" Holding Center, I took a look around, wondering if I would be brought back there after my court appearance.

The next thing I knew I was arriving at the "Broward County Jail" building in downtown Ft. Lauderdale.

I was taken up to the 5TH floor, which was the "maximum-security" floor that the Broward County Sheriff rented out to the "F.B.I".!

They keep the lights on 24 hours a day, 7 days a week, and watch you continuously with video cameras!

There were fourteen other prisoners in the "cell-block" besides me, being held on many different charges, including murder!

As far as "exercise" was concerned, they took us to the "roof area", which was fenced in, every other day, for two hours of sunshine.

After going up there several times, I noticed that they had an old officer that was about sixty years old, that was watching over us for the "recreation" period.

I also noticed very quickly that he was armed with a .357 magnum pistol in a holster.

I then noticed that some of the guys who went to recreation usually spent time talking to the old officer, and that when they were talking to him, he wasn't watching me very much.

So, I started planning again to "escape"! This time from the "Broward County Jail"!

Now, each time we were taken up to 5th floor, I began working on a corner of the fence, to make an opening big enough for me to get through

My plan was to get through the fence, jump from the 5th floor down to the 1ST floor cage, and jump to the ground!

From there I could disappear into the crowd, find someone with a car, and I'd be "home free"!

I was determined to "escape", or die trying!

I had received training in the military on how run away and dodge bullets when someone was shooting at you, and "escape" was the "only" thing that occupied my mind at the time!

I knew that if I was convicted of First Degree Murder and Kidnapping, that I would be sent to sit in Florida's electric chair, and be "executed"!

# CHAPTER 12

## "Saved By The Hand Of God"
### June 1987

As I waited in my cell for my sentencing date, I stayed in constant prayer to my "Lord", asking Him to watch over me, and my "loved" ones that were in Miami for the trial.

Then, one week after being found guilty something "amazing" happened!

One morning, out of the "clear blue", they called my name for a visit.

But, as I went down to the visiting area, I noticed that this visit was "special"! Not only was the visit "unexpected", but it was to be a "contact" visit in a room, instead of through "bulletproof" glass on a telephone handset!

As I found out, there were two gentleman there to see me.

They introduced themselves as Mr. Paul Green, and his assistant was named Mr. Damian Pacca.

"Mr. Castillo, we belong to an organization that fights against the "death penalty", and we would like to represent you at your sentencing hearing, if this would be alright with you", they said to me.

"But, I do not have any money to hire any more lawyers for my case", I replied.

"You do not have to pay us, Juan Pablo. The organization that we work for pays our salary". they said.

"We fight against the death sentence, a we believe that they should "abolish" it is favor of "life" sentences, which we believe is much more humane of a 'civilized' society".

"Well, in that case, what do I have to do"? I asked them.

"Juan Pablo, when you next go in front of the Judge, tell him that you have hired me to represent you in the penalty phase of the trial. We'll take it from there", they said.

And that is what we did do at the next hearing.

After Judge Di Gennaro entered, and was seated behind the bench, I had my original attorney, "Smith Jones", inform the Judge that I had hired new counsel to now represent me in the penalty phase, and that his name is "Mr. Paul Green", with his assistant, "Mr. Damian Pacca"".

The Judge then asked:

"Mr. Green, how much time do you need to be ready for the penalty phase of Mr. Castillo' trial"?

Mr. Green then approached the bench and said that we would need thirty days to prepare.

"Make it 'twenty' days, Mr. Green which is three weeks from today. That should be sufficient for you to prepare, sir"! said Judge Di Gennaro in a "booming" voice.

"Agreed, your Honor", replied my new attorney.

The Judge then addressed the "States Attorney", which is what Florida calls its "District Attorney" here, and said

"Mr. Laser, it is the order of this court that you will assist Mr. Green with all that he needs from your office to prepare for the penalty phase of this trial.

"That will include opening the Law Library for their research purposes. Is that clear, sir"?

"Perfectly clear, your Honor"!

Then, Judge Di Gennaro turned to Mr. Green and stated:

"Mr. Green, you will have to convince me as to why I should not follow the recommendation of the jury, and the laws of the great state of Florida, and sentence Mr. Castillo to death by electric chair for the crimes he has been found guilty of by this court."

"Yes, your Honor", answered Mr. Green "That is my intention, sir"!

We then met again for a visit, after court was adjourned, to plan our strategy for the next hearing in three weeks.

After being called out for an attorney visit, Mr. Green told me that we needed some people that knew me well to appear at the next hearing on my behalf.

"Juan Pablo, I need some members of your "family", that witnessed your abuse as a child, so that I can put them on the stand. The jury has recommended to the Judge that you should receive a sentence of "death" in this case, and it falls on me now to convince him otherwise. Who can you think of that we can bring to court that would be willing to testify on your behalf?"

"Well, my sister "Luz" is already here, and attended the trial with me. I have another sister, "Consuelo", and I'm sure that she'll come if we bring her over from Colombia." I have a friend from El-Reno Prison in Oklahoma, "Anthony Doyle", of Anthony Doyle Ministries. "Also, my mother's sister, my aunt "Adelphia". She always tried to stop the beatings when she could. She'll probably come too, as will our neighbor, "Rosio", who lived across the street from us," I said.

"Good, Juan Pablo. This is exactly what we need! A will fly to Colombia in a few days and speak to them for you. The court will pay for their transportation and lodging if necessary. "Please give me their 'contact' information, for when I arrive there," said Mr. Green.

_ _ _ _ _ _ _ _ _ _ _ _ _ _ _ _ _ _

In the meantime, while Mr. Green flew to "Medellin", Colombia; I made myself useful, looking up 'case law' for him in the law library. But, I could find nothing of use

The "Lord God" had promised me that I would not be "executed", and I have "full faith" in his promise that this is true, as I know that "God" does not lie!

_ _ _ _ _ _ _ _ _ _ _ _ _ _ _ _ _ _

Several days later, Mr. Green returned from Colombia, and with him came my sister "Consuelo", and her two sons, my "nephew"

My Cousin; "Luz Stella", also came for me, and my mother's sister, my aunt "Adelphia", along with our neighbor from across the street, "Rosio Sanchez".

I was so surprised, and amazed, to see these members of my family, and my neighbor, that knew of my childhood in Colombia. Also these to testify was "Black Williams," my Christian mentor from El-Reno. We were allowed to have a "special" visit, and I busted out in tears as I was hugged and kissed by my sisters, my cousin, my nephews, and my aunt "Adelphia", along with "Rosio", our neighbor

It had been so long since I had seen them and we had so much to talk about. My nephews, "Carolina 6 yrs. old and Miuricio 9 yrs. old, gave me so many, many hugs and kisses, and told me how much they loved their "Uncle Juan Pablo".

"Juan Pablo", they all said tearfully, "they're going to execute you"!

"There is no way that you're going to escape from here, 'Juan Pablo', or avoid getting the death penalty for this"!

I then told them: "I have asked "God" for nothing, yet He made me three promises. He told me that He is going to spare my "life", and I will not be "executed" in the electric chair. "God" does not lie to me, or anyone, and I "believe and have total "faith" in God's word, and His promise to me"!

"I am telling you this before it happens, so that you too will 'believe' in God's power"!

"And when it 'happens' in that courtroom, you 'will' be a 'believer'!"

They all started shaking their heads in exasperation, mumbling to themselves how crazy and shot out, and "out there" I was.

They were all crying as they got up to leave after the visit, but I was determined to stay strong in my "faith", and believe in Gods promises to me. I hugged them all again, and told them to keep me in their prayers each night.

— — — — — — — — — — — — — — — — — —

I called them daily, and told them of my faith in my "Lord," and of His saving grace and forgiveness of my sins.

— — — — — — — — — — — — — — — — — —

June 26, 1987

The twenty days passed by too quickly, and the date of my sentencing hearing arrived.

I got up from my bunk, got down on my knees, and began to pray to the "Lord" for strength, as I knew that the testimony from my family and friends would be emotional, and I did not want to break down in the courtroom.

I took a shower, "shaved," and put on an all – "black" jail uniform. After being convicted at trial, they no longer allowed me to wear my suit to court. My shirt, pants and slip-on shoes were dark black.

The jailer came to get me, and again I was handcuffed and chained up hand and foot like a "wild" animal that they needed to keep under control.

I did not let this bother me, as my mind was on my "Lord," and my heart went out to my relatives, who had come so far from Colombia for me. I love them so very much.

As we approached the courtroom, several "T. reporters attempted to get close to me, to ask questions on "live" television cameras covering the sentencing hearing. They were stopped by armed deputies before they could get to me.

As I was escorted into the courtroom, I looked around at all of the people sitting in their seats. They had all turned around, and were now staring directly at me.

From one side of the courtroom, I could feel the "searing" heat of hatred as the friends and family of the victim stared me down with their eyes, wishing me to be dead already.

As I walked toward the defense table at the front of the courtroom, I saw my sisters, "Luz and Consuelo," sitting next to each other, along with my cousins "Luz Stella" and my Aunt Adelphia. My neighbor, "Rosio", sat next to them also.

They smiled at me through teary eyes, and threw me kisses as they said; "I love you, Juan Pablo".

It was all I could do to keep my composure as I passed by them before taking my seat next to my attorney, Mr. Green; and his assistant, Mr. Damian Pacca.

We all stood as Judge Di Gennaro entered and took his seat behind the bench.

"This court is now in session", Judge Di Gennaro stated in a "booming" voice, as he banged his gassel down hard!

"Mr. Green, are you ready"? asked the Judge, as he looked over at us at the defense table.

"Yes, your Honor", replied my attorney.

"You May Proceed," stated Judge Di Gennaro, as he leaned back in his chair.

"Thank you, your Honor"! said Green as he stood up from the defense table, and walked up before the bench.

"Judge Di Gennaro, I ask you to look at the defendant, my client; "Juan Pablo Castillo", and imagine him if you will, not as an 'adult' sitting before you, but as a 'child'"!

"I ask you, your Honor, to judge him not as an 'adult' here today, but as a 'child' going through his life being "horrendously" abused by the very people that he trusts, the people who he looked up to, the very people that he counted on for love and protection and support as a child?

"I ask this of you, your Honor, because what happened to Juan Pablo as a child affected him for the rest of his "life"!" "It affected him deeply as he grew up into a man"!

"Please listen to these witnesses that I am about to put on the stand, your "Honor", and I ask you to take into account what they have to say of Juan Pablo's childhood, and the horrific violence he endured at his young age, as his very 'life' hangs in the balance of their testimony".

"Thank you, your Honor".

"As my first witness, I call to the stand Mr. Anthony Doyle."

(Clerk of court) "Mr. Williams, do you swear to tell the truth, the whole truth, and nothing but the truth, so help you God"?

(Williams) "I do".

(Green) "Mr. Williams, please tell the court how you come to meet Juan Pablo Castillo".

(Williams) "I met Juan Pablo at the El-Reno Federal Correction Institution in El-Reno, Oklahoma; in 1985 when he arrived from "Los Angeles", California.

(Green) "And where was it that you met him"?

(Williams) "We met in the Chapel there".

(Green) "What was Juan Pablo doing in the Chapel"?

(Williams) "He was talking to the Chaplain about the "Christian" program that were available there, and introducing himself to the Christian community there".

(McG.) "What was his demeanor, sir? By that I mean his general attitude and behavior toward other inmates there"!

(Williams) "His demeanor was calm, almost docile. He was very "excited" about the Chapel, and wanted to learn all he could about Jesus, our "savior", the son of God".

(McG.) "You said "our" savior. Are you also a "Christian", Mr. Williams"?

(Williams) "Yes sir, I am. I am an ordained minister now, and a "born-again" Christian"

(McG.) "I see, and you had gotten to know Juan Pablo pretty well while he was there at El-Reno, am I correct?"

(Williams) "I became his "mentor". He was like a brother to me".

(McG.) "Like a 'brother'. In what ways?"

(Williams) "We went everywhere in the prison together. Not only to 'Chapel,' but we ate our meals together most of the time, talked about life, and confided our problems to each other. If he did not understand something that he had read in the Bible, I would put it in the proper content so that he could better understand what it meant."

(McG.) "So, you were a kind of a teacher to Juan Pablo, then?"

(Williams) "Yes, a teacher, but also a trusted friend and counselor".

(McG.) "Was Juan Pablo just curious about Jesus, and the books of the Bible?"

(Williams) "No sir! Juan Pablo was on "fire" for Jesus! I have never met anyone who was as "hungry" for the word of 'God' as he is!

"Whenever he met someone, he began relating how much he loved the Lord, and how all sinners can be forgiven if they'll repent and accept Jesus as their Lord and Savior!"

Sir, Juan Pablo did not seek out "religion"! God grabbed Juan Pablo, stopped him dead in his tracks from trying to escape, and turned him 'inside out'

(McG.) "So, Mr. Williams, you would know it then if Juan Pablo were trying to "fake it" just to get people to believe that he had changed?"

(Williams) "You cannot fool a true Christian? I would be able to tell very quickly if a person were trying to "fake it," as no one can fool you 24 hours a day, 7 days a week, and 365 days a year, as there would be moments when the true character of that person came out, when they let their guard down. I never saw any of that with Juan Pablo".

(McG.) "So, you believe that Juan Pablo Castillo is a true "born again" Christian?"

(Williams) "Mr. Green, I have never in my life met a man so dedicated to the 'Lord,' and so fervent in his beliefs and in his faith in 'God'! I know that Juan Pablo is a "true believer", and an upstanding "Christian" man, and I would not only trust him with my own 'life', but also with the very 'lives' of my entire family!"

(McG.) "So you believe his faith is real?"

(Williams) "Yes, I do! You cannot "fake" the kind of faith Juan Pablo has. He was always in prayer, whenever and wherever I saw him. If ever there was a "true-believer", Juan Pablo is that person. I have no doubt about it"!

(McG.) "How did Juan Pablo deal with". . . .

"IF HE'S SO GOOD OF A 'CHRISTIAN', LET HIM DIE AND GO TO HEAVEN"! (yelled a spectator "sarcastically" from the victim's side of the courtroom)!

(Judge Di Gennaro) "There will be order in this court"... Judge Di Gennaro stated in his "booming" voice

"One more outburst like that and I will clear this courtroom for the remainder of this hearing"! stated Judge Di Gennaro as he banged his gavel down repeatedly!

(Judge Di Gennaro) "You may continue, Mr. Williams".

(Williams) – "Thank you, your Honor".

"Mr. Green, could you please repeat the last question?"

(McG.) "Of course. How did "Juan Pablo Castillo" deal with the violent episodes that he encountered there at "El-Reno" Prison?"

(Williams) "Juan Pablo was very much respected there at El-Reno, both as a Christian man that could be trusted, and as a man with good character and good leadership abilities, both by staff members and other inmates".

"Juan Pablo would see some trouble brewing, and he would attempt to mediate a solutions to keep things from getting out of hand and turning violent! I had lost count of how many times Juan Pablo stepped into the middle of a potential gang fight, and stopped it from happening".

(McG.) "Thank you, Mr. Williams".

"Your Honor, I have no further questions for this witness".

(Judge Di Gennaro) "Mr. Williams, you may step down, sir".

"Mr. Green, you may call your next witness".

(McG.) "I now call Miss "Adelphia Garcia" to the stand".

(Judge Di Gennaro) "Having been sworn in, you may proceed".

(McG.) "Adelphia, please tell the court your relationship to Juan Pablo Castillo".

(Adelphia) "I am Juan Pablo's Aunt, his mother's sister".

(McG.) "Adelphia, please tell the court about Juan Pablo's life as a young child, as you remember it".

(Adelphia) (Breaks down in tears.)

(Judge Di Gennaro) "It's ok, ma'am, take your time".

(Adelphia) "Well, when Juan Pablo was a young boy, his father put both him, and his younger brother, in a Military Academy School".

"His father was very strict with him, and would make him obey his orders like he was a soldier"!

"He wasn't allowed to go out and play like other children, and his room had to be absolutely "spotless" all of the time. It was like he was to be an "adult," and was not allowed to have a "childhood" like other children".

(McG.) "Can you tell us of any traumatic events in his early years, that may have affected him badly?"

(Adelphia) – "Yes! He was very badly affected by his father abandoning him and his family for another woman. He had "idolized" his father, and loved him very much, and when his father left without even saying goodbye, "I love you", to Juan Pablo or any of them, it totally devastated Juan Pablo, and overwhelmed him emotionally. He was in total shock"!

"His father had left them with no money for food, or bills that needed to be paid, and Juan Pablo's mother had to sell their furniture, and personal possessions, and leave the house they had lived in, moving all of them into a single room that she rented."

(McG.) "How did this effect Juan Pablo?"

(Adelphia) "He was very sad, and thought very strongly that he was to blame in some way, which he wasn't."

(McG.) "How did your sister, Juan Pablo's mother, react to being abandoned like that?"

(Adelphia) "At first she just cried a lot. Then she found work sewing for a wealthy family, where she was allowed to bring home some "left-over" food for her and the children to eat."

"Juan Pablo's friends found out that he didn't have a dad anymore and that Juan Pablo was eating rich people's "left-overs", and they started making fun of him and his brother and sisters, which led to fights where Juan Pablo stood up for them. Juan Pablo was totally "humiliated", and became very sad and depress

"Juan Pablo's mother took out her anger on him very "violently", first spanking him a lot with a thick belt, then hitting him with her hands and fists, then using 2 x 4 boards to hit him with. His mother totally changed into another person, one that was consumed with hate and anger, which she released on Juan Pablo."

(Breaks down crying again)

(Judge Di Gennaro) "Would you like a few moments to compose yourself"?

(Adelphia) "No, your Honor. I'm ok now."

(Judge Di Gennaro) "Please continue, ma'am".

(Adelphia) "My sister totally turned on Juan Pablo, and several times almost drowned him, once in a large tub of water."

"I saw Juan Pablo begin to change from an obedient child who would do anything he was told to do, into a rebellious child, both at home and at school."

"Juan Pablo ended up taking to the streets to get away from his mothers violent temper and the beatings she was giving him, and he took up with the "street people", criminals and prostitutes, as they didn't try to hurt him like his mother did".

(McG.) "Did you ever try to stop your sister from beating Juan Pablo"?

(Adelphia) "Yes, I tried to intervene many times, but I was not successful."

"My sister always told me to mind my own business, and don't get involved".

"She said that Juan Pablo was her son, and she'll raise him, and deal with him, her way."

(McG.) "Which was very "violently"?

(Adelphia) "Yes, sir"!

(McG.) "Your Honor, I have no further questions for this witness".

(Judge Di Gennaro) – "You may step down, ma'am, thank you".

"Mr. Green, you may call your next witness".

(McG.) "Your Honor, I now call "Rosio Sanchez" to the stand".

(Judge Di Gennaro) "Having been sworn in, you may proceed".

(McG.) "Mrs. Sanchez, please tell the court how you know Juan Pablo Castillo".

(Rosio) "I lived across the street from then when Juan Pablo was a young boy".

(McG.) "How well did you know Juan Pablo? Did you just see him out in front of his house, or did you get to know him better than that?"

(Rosio) "OH, I got to know little Juan Pablo very well. His family lived across the street from me for several years, and Juan Pablo would stop by and talk to me all the time".

(McG.) "Did you ever have any occasion of witnessing any violence directed towards Juan Pablo, while he lived across the street from you?"

(Rosio) "Yes sir, many times"!

(McG.) "Would you please tell the court what you witnessed, Mrs. Sanchez"?

(Rosio) "Yes, of course. After Juan Pablo's dad left the family and abandoned them, Juan Pablo became very depressed and sad. His mother was highly upset, and angry, and yelled at Juan Pablo for any little thing. Sometimes for no reason at all."

"I remember that I heard about some coins from his mother's employer that came up missing, and Juan Pablo's brother said 'he'd' taken them, and took him to the movie theater with him."

"When Juan Pablo's mother found out about it, she almost beat Juan Pablo to death"!

"His mother's employer's son had to kick the bedroom door down and pull Juan Pablo's mother off of Juan Pablo, as he was bloody and bruised, and barely breathing." "She had a knife in her hand"!

"Juan Pablo came over to my house, and I cleaned his wounds and gave him something to eat, as he was starving. I also counseled him about things that he shouldn't do, so that he wouldn't set his mother off, but it didn't matter, as his mother was always taking out her anger on little Juan Pablo, whether he had done anything or not. She was complete off the chain"!

(McG.) "Was that the only time he'd came over to your house all 'beaten' up"?

(Rosio) "No, sir! It had only gotten worse, especially after he started hanging around on the streets with the street people."

"His mother had forbidden him to leave the house, but whenever she would beat him again, he would leave the house and come back days later", which would lead to another beating, where he would leave again!"

"Juan Pablo began to drink on the street, and use drugs."

(McG.) "Did Juan Pablo ever see his father again?"

(Rosio) "Yes, I believe it was about a year later when his father showed up again on their doorstep, when they had moved in with Juan Pablo's grandmother".

(McG.) "Did the beatings stop after Juan Pablo's father came back home to live"?

(Rosio) "No sir, not in the least"!

(McG.) "Why is that? The family was back together again".

(Rosio) "Mr. Green, Juan Pablo's father was a very bad alcoholic"!

(McG.) "I see, and was there tension between Juan Pablo and his father after he'd returned home to live"?

(Rosio) "OH, Yes! Juan Pablo's father pretty much stayed drunk most of the time, and when Juan Pablo came home from the streets, his father would order him around and beat him himself!"

"When his dad returned home, he acted like he'd never left, and thought that Juan Pablo was going to become the "little soldier" again.

"But Juan Pablo's "love" for his father had turned to "hate" after he'd abandoned them, and Juan Pablo had no more respect left for his father, so Juan Pablo rebelled against him."

"Juan Pablo's father then began to beat Juan Pablo mercilessly, tying him up and hanging him by his feet upside down and setting a fire under his head, which burned his hair off and made burns and blisters on his head and neck. I myself cleaned him up after that, and put some ointment on his burns."

(McG.) "So, Juan Pablo's father had turned into a very angry, violent alcoholic, and turned his anger against Juan Pablo also?"

(Rosio) "Yes, sir"!

(McG.) "Did you ever try to intervene"?

(Rosio) "Yes, I fought with Juan Pablo's mother many a time, telling her that one day she's going to kill Juan Pablo, but she wouldn't listen, and kept telling me to mind my own business, and stay out of hers"!

(McG.) "I see. Thank you, Mrs. Sanchez."

"Your Honor, I have no further questions for this witness".

(Judge Di Gennaro) — "Mrs. Sanchez, you may step down, ma'am, and thank you".

"Mr. Green, you may call your next witness".

(McG.) "I now call Mrs. Consuelo Garcia to the stand".

(Judge Di Gennaro) "Having been duly sworn in, you may proceed".

(McG.) "Please state your name, and your relationship to Juan Pablo Castillo".

(Consuelo) (STARTS CRYING OUT LOUD UNCONTROLLABLY)

(Judge Di Gennaro) "Take your time, it's ok".

AFTER A FEW MOMENTS

(Consuelo) – "Thank you, your Honor".

"My name is Consuelo Garcia, and I am Juan Pablo's sister."

(McG.) "Mrs. Garcia, please tell the court of your memories of Juan Pablo's childhood."

(Consuelo) "Well, Juan Pablo was a sweet boy, and a good brother to me. He was the oldest of my two brothers, and he was always looking out for the rest of us when we were young. He would not let anyone hurt us, or talk bad to us in any way whatsoever".

"As a child, Juan Pablo was my dad's little "soldier", and Juan Pablo loved dad a lot, and wanted to be just like him. It seemed to Juan Pablo that our father was the 'smartest' man in the world."

"Juan Pablo was very smart as a child, and he dreamed of going to college, and medical school, so that he could study to become a doctor, a 'surgeon' really."

(McG.) "Juan Pablo wanted to become a 'surgeon'"?

(Consuelo) "Yes, sir! He saw so much sickness in the world, and sick people everywhere, and he wanted so much to be able to heal them, and make them well again"!

"He told me many times that dad told him that he could be anything that he wanted to be, if he tried hard enough".

(McG.) "So, Juan Pablo wanted to heal the sick people of the world?"

(Consuelo) "OH, Yes! Juan Pablo was very serious about becoming a surgeon! He used to go out in our backyard and chase little green lizards"!

"When he caught them, he would put them on his little "operating table" he'd made. Then, he would "scrub-up" really good, to get the germs off of his hands, and he'd then use alcohol to sterilize his surgical instruments, which were a small razor blade from dad's safety razor, gauze, some cotton balls, and a sewing needle and thread to stitch them up after surgery".

(McG.)– "After surgery?!"

"He 'operated' on the 'lizards'?!"

(Consuelo) "OH, Yes! All the time! It was very important to him that all of his 'patients', the lizards, be very healthy and happy in our backyard!"

(McG.) "I see. That is 'fascinating', Mrs. Garcia."

"May I ask you, what, in your memories of his childhood, kept Juan Pablo from realizing his dream of becoming a 'surgical' doctor?"

(Consuelo) "I believe with all my heart that the turning point in his life was when our dad left, and 'abandoned' mom and all of us kids to move in with another woman".

"It was totally 'devastating' to Juan Pablo, as he had look up to dad so much." "Juan Pablo then believed he had no future, and lost 'focus' in his life, and his dreams turned to ashes and were gone"

"When dad left, and mom had to sell all of the furniture and personal items, and we were all moved into a rented room, Juan Pablo lost all respect and love for our dad."

"He couldn't believe that dad could do something like that to us, and it hurt him 'profoundly'! I believe it damaged him very deeply, 'psychologically', as he never got over it, even after dad came home".

(McG.) "Did you yourself witness any violence directed at Juan Pablo as a child?"

(Consuelo) "Yes! So many times I couldn't count them."

(McG.) "Please tell this court what you saw, 'ma'am'".

(Consuelo) "Well, it started after dad moved out."

"Juan Pablo took some coins, and took his little brother to the movies, and bought popcorn, candy & sodas with them."

(Consuelo) "When mom found out about it, she quite literally tried to beat little Juan Pablo to death over it, and would have killed him if she had not been stopped that day!"

"Then, even when Juan Pablo was acting like any other ten year old boy, by running in the house, or knocking over a 'potted' plant, or something like that, mom would just completely 'lose' it, and go violently "insane" with hate"!

"To mom, if she couldn't make Juan Pablo change with a 'spanking', she would hit him repeatedly, over and over and over again with her "fists", and hands!"

"She then tried boards, and would hit little Juan Pablo on the head a lot of times, making him really bloody with lots of cuts and gashes."

"She almost beat him to death once".

"Also, she tried to drown him several times. She had just completely changed into another person after dad left us!"

(McG.) "How did all of Juan Pablo's brothers and sisters get along with Juan Pablo?"

(Consuelo) "Great! We all loved Juan Pablo very much, as he was our 'biggest' brother, and our protector"!

"Many times Juan Pablo would go out into the streets and come back with money, which he would spend on all of us kids. Sometimes he would take all of us to the movies at the theater, and buy us candy and popcorn and sodas and such. He was always looking out for us".

(McG.) "So, to sum up how you feel about Juan Pablo, your "biggest" brother, you would say what?"

(Consuelo) "Juan Pablo is a very fine brother, that anyone would want to have, and he is a good person. He is a man with a heart of gold"!

(McG.) "Consuelo, is there anything else you would like to say to this court about Juan Pablo?"

(Consuelo) "Yes"! (Starts to cry.) "Please don't kill Juan Pablo. I love him very much, and I need him. We all do"!

(McG.) "Your Honor, I have no further questions for this witness".

(Judge Di Gennaro) "You may step down now, and thank you".

(McG.) "Your Honor, I now call my last witness to the stand, Mrs. "Luz Garcia".

(Judge Di Gennaro) "Having been duly sworn, you may proceed."

(McG.) "Mrs. Garcia, please tell the court your relationship to Juan Pablo Castillo".

(Luz)– "Juan Pablo Castillo is my brother"….and….

(Luz)– "OH, GOD"!

(BREAKS DOWN COMPLETELY AND STARTS CRYING)

(Luz) "OH, God! Please, please don't kill my brother, Please;" (CRYING UNCONTROLLABLY)!

"Please don't kill Juan Pablo, Please God,"

"OH, God!"

"Please don't kill him, Judge"!

(BREAKS DOWN COMPLETELY, EMOTIONALLY)!!!

(Judge Di Gennaro) "Mr. Green, would you like a short recess, so that your witness can compose herself?"

(McG.) "Your Honor, if it please the court. I believe Mrs. Garcia has shown this court her feelings about her brother, 'Juan Pablo Castillo', and the possible penalty that he is facing here today."

"I have no further questions for Mrs. Luz Garcia, your Honor".

(Judge Di Gennaro) – "This witness is excused, and may step down. Thank you, Mrs. Garcia".

(Luz) "I am so sorry, Judge"!!

(McG.) "Thank you, your Honor".

(Judge Di Gennaro) "Mr. Green, you may begin your closing argument at this time".

(Green) "Thank you, your Honor".

"Three weeks ago today, your Honor, you told me that I would need to convince you as to why you should not follow the jury's recommendation, and sentence Juan Pablo Castillo to death."

"Today, your Honor, I am going to try to meet that burden, as Juan Pablo's life hangs in the balance."

"Your Honor, this morning, at the beginning of this hearing, I asked you not to look at Juan Pablo Castillo as an 'adult,' but to look at him as a 'child'."

"Today, I asked you not to "judge" him as an adult, but to judge him as a child also, one going through life being terribly abused by the very people that he looked up to, the ones that should have been 'loving' him and 'protecting' him. The people that he trusted with his very 'life', sir. His 'parents'".

"I asked this of you, your Honor, because, as I said before, what happened to Juan Pablo as a 'child' affected him dramatically as he was growing up and becoming a man!"

"I believe, your Honor, that from the witnesses that have testified here today before this court, that it has seen the 'horror' of the abuse that Juan Pablo endured as a young boy, and the 'violence' that was part of his young life".

"As we have heard from the witnesses' testimony here today, Juan Pablo's 'father', the person loved and looked up to the most by Juan Pablo, 'abandoned' him, and his mother, brother and sisters for another woman at a time when little Juan Pablo was 'dreaming' of, and aspiring to study to become a future 'surgeon', so that he could heal the sick people of the world, a dream of joining a profession that is revered, respected, and 'honored' the world over"!

"As we have also heard through testimony here in this courtroom today, your Honor, that because of our event beyond the control of a young child, 'little Juan Pablo Castillo', the abandonment of the family by the father and sole provides, that this traumatic event caused Juan Pablo's mother to turn 'insanely' violent, completely changing her into another person, a person filled with hate, bitterness and violent tendencies toward little Juan Pablo".

"I ask you, your Honor, to take into account here today, the 'extremely' horrible effect that this abandonment, and violence, had on young Juan Pablo Castillo".

"I ask you, your Honor, to understand that this was not just a 'few' violent episodes in his life, but was 'excessive' violence directed at him almost 'daily'".

"Making the situation worse, your Honor, was the fact that Juan Pablo's father had become an extremely violent alcoholic".

"We have heard in this courtroom today, that, because of the 'abandonment' of his family, and because of the theft of a few 'coins' by a young child used to go to the theater with his brother, that it set in motion a streak of violence against Juan Pablo that quite literally forced him to flee, and leave home and go into the streets to get away from the 'horrific' violence being directed against him at home, so as not to be possibly killed by his own parents."

"We have heard here today of young Juan Pablo turning to both alcohol and drugs at a very young age, to 'blunt' the hurt and anger he felt because of the violent treatment he was receiving at home."

"We have seen that his young life was filled with misery, hate and violence, not happiness, love and protection."

"Your Honor, please imagine the damage, both physical and psychological and emotional, that little Juan Pablo received as a young boy, and of Juan Pablo turning to the people he befriended on the streets, the thugs, prostitutes and other criminals, the ones that we see partly raised him, who gave him comfort where he did not receive any at home. They cared more for Juan Pablo then his own parents did!"

"Your Honor, I ask you now to read, and to take into account here today, the state ordered 'psychological' report from the testing done on Mr. Castillo".

"Your Honor, according to the report, as I read it "verbatim", it states that:"

"The alcohol and drug use, and extremely violent childhood endured by Juan Pablo Castillo was a "lethal combination", which caused young Juan Pablo to literally lose his "innocent" mind, and contributed to the diminishing of his moral, right way of thinking, affecting him as he grew up, the effect of which caused him to act out "aggressively", and become a violent individual as an adult".

## (CONCLUSION)

"In conclusion, your Honor, I ask this court to seek "justice" for Juan Pablo Castillo the "child", not revenge, your Honor, as "any" child in the world raised in that 'horrendous' climate of violence, alcohol and drugs, is in danger of becoming violent"!

"There are too many individuals in prisons today that never even had a chance at a normal childhood because of these same circumstances in life!"

"Today, your Honor, I ask you to take into account the entire "scope" of abuse that Juan Pablo endured as a young boy, abuse that no child on "earth" should ever have to experience in their childhood".

## (CLOSING)

"In closing, your Honor, I also believe that by the testimony we have heard here today in this courtroom, that it has been shown that Juan Pablo Castillo, the "adult", has experienced a "rebirth" of character, "born" of a faith in "God", our creator!"

"Your Honor, please note that Juan Pablo Castillo was not seeking religion, yet "God" found Juan Pablo, stopped him dead in his tracks from going through with a planned escape, and turned him "inside out" into another person entirely, the one you see here before you today".

"Your Honor, it would be a travesty and an injustice to Juan Pablo Castillo the "child", to execute Juan Pablo Castillo the "adult"!"

"As my last statement to this court today, your Honor, I ask you to make the right decision, and let justice and mercy prevail against hatred and revenge. I ask you, Judge Di Gennaro, to spare the life of Juan Pablo Castillo".

"Thank you, your Honor".

"I rest my case at this time, sir".

"The life of Juan Pablo Castillo rests in your hands".

(Judge Di Gennaro) "Mr. Green, have you found any "case law" that would show me as to why I shouldn't execute this man"?

(McG.) "Your Honor, there is no case law on the books pertaining as to why not, but there is "case law" that was just handed down yesterday by the United States Supreme Court."

5:00 PM

"You can have that "case law" faxed to your chambers if necessary, your Honor".

(Judge Di Gennaro) "I will be back with my decision in three hours. This court is adjourned."

(Juan Pablo) I then turned around in my seat at the defense table and saw the victim's family and friends staring hard at me, mouthing obscenities.

As I looked behind me at my sisters, "Luz and Consuelo," I felt the warmth of the love that they felt for me at that moment. It was very very comforting to me.

My Aunt "Adelphia" blew me kisses, as did my cousin, "Luz Stella". I was so happy and thankful to God for them being there for me.

They took me back through the tunnel to the jail, and back to my cellblock, to await the Judge's decision.

I am praying in my cell, and I felt the Lord telling me to open my Bible.

I open it to the book of "Revelations", and my eyes stop on Chapter 12, and verse 11 A, which say:

("Revelation" Chap. 12:11A) "And they overcame him by the blood of the Lamb and by the word of their testimony".

I smile as I read these words, as I know that it is my "Lord" Jesus, my savior, reassuring me that He is with me in the courtroom, and always, and that His promise to me will prevail. I am praying, my family and friends are praying, everyone is praying for me tonight.

(8:56 pm) I am told by an officer to get ready to go, as they are taking me back to the courtroom.

We started walking back through the tunnel connecting the jail to the courthouse, and were on our way to the courtroom, when I noticed a large pile of wires, little television monitors, and a large amount of reporters in the hallways leading into the courtroom.

I figured that they were going to both go "live" on television, and record the proceedings for later playback, like it was something everyone should see.

As we went inside the courtroom, I noticed that the "setting" of the courtroom was completely different now.

Now, between the Judge's bench and the courtroom "spectators", there were over a "dozen" armed police officers, "fanned" out in a 'semicircle', standing 'shoulder to shoulder', to protect the Judge from being attacked.

They were watching everyone very closely, and even had deputies checking people coming into the courtroom, patting them down and using metal detector wands on them, to check for possible weapons. I had never seen anything like it before.

We sat down at the defense table, and I turned to see my sister, "Luz", sitting behind me. I said "I love you" to her just as she burst into tears, crying uncontrollably.

I smiled at her, and told her not to worry, which made her cry even harder.

Several minutes later we all stood as the Judge entered the courtroom.

What happened next was really, really "ugly"!

The Judge addressed the courtroom with these words:

(Judge Di Gennaro) "Ladies and Gentleman, in the United States of America, in many cases, lives have been spared from execution"

"In Mr. Castillo's case, I found two 'aggravating' circumstances".

"The first being the way the victim was killed, and the second being the premeditation of the murder".

"I then found two mitigating circumstances that are equally powerful"!

"The first one being the horrific abuse young Juan Pablo went through as a boy, as we heard the witnesses testify to here in this courtroom today"

"The second being that he was under the influence of both drugs and alcohol at the time these crimes were committed, as the witnesses from the government testified to also."

(Judge Di Gennaro) "So this is my final decision"!

(Juan Pablo) It became so "quiet" in the courtroom that you could have heard a "piss" drop, and the air was filled with both tension and hopefulness as the Judge spoke these final words:

(Judge Di Gennaro) "I hereby sentence you to "25 years in prison"!

"I am sparing Juan Pablo Castillo's life"!

(Juan Pablo) As those last words were spoken by the Judge, there was an "explosion" of emotions taking place as the courtroom erupted like a "volcano" in anger and frustration!

   Some of the victim's friends and family made threats towards Judge Di Gennaro, asking "where was the justice in allowing me to live?"

One of them yelled out: saying

"Now the people are pulling the cart with the oxen in it, instead of the oxen pulling the cart!"

Another "screamed" out: saying

"We're going to make sure that you're not going to be a "Judge" in our county anymore"!

   Then, on the other side of the courtroom, my family and church friends were praying and thanking the "Lord" for sparing my life!

(Juan Pablo) The next thing I noticed was that the police had surrounded the Judge and were taking him out of the courtroom.

They then surrounded my family and church members, and escorted them out of the courtroom under armed guard for their safety.

They then surrounded me, & escorted me out of the courtroom and into the tunnel & back to the jail!

As I was watching the television news in my cellblock later that night, I saw that Judge Di Gennaro was being interviewed on the news show, "Inside Edition"!

When the reporter asked the Judge why he didn't follow the recommendation of the jury and sentence me to death, Judge Di Gennaro replied:

(Judge Di Gennaro) "I believe that his faith is real"! "But, as I was in my chambers, I was sure that I was going to sentence him to death, but, as soon as I returned to this courtroom, something changed my mind".

(Judge Di Gennaro) "It was like there was a power that came over me that would not let me sign his death sentence"!

"I can't really explain it, other than that"!

(Juan Pablo) I then saw my sister, "Luz", being interviewed, and she was crying uncontrollably as the reporter asked her how she felt about the Judge's decision to spare my life.

She couldn't speak! She was "dumbfounded", as she fully expected me to receive the death sentence from Judge Di Gennaro!

(Juan Pablo) The next day in the "Miami Herald", the front page screamed:

"Castillo Saved By A Miracle"!

(Juan Pablo) Some members of my family left after the Judge's decision, and went back to Colombia.

One of my cousins, "Stella", stayed for awhile to visit with me before returning to New York.

My sister, "Luz Garcia", told me that she was going to stay by my side, regardless of what is going to happen, because when she dies she wants to be buried next to me.

After I was sent to Levenworth Federal Penitentiary, she returned to New York.

Because of "God" and my sister, "Luz", I have been able to survive in this "jungle".

Three weeks later, "Judge Steve Di Gennaro" was removed from the "bench"!

I sat smiling as I openly thanked my "Lord" for His precious promises to me. As I read my Bible that night, I heard my Lord's voice in my head, and felt Him in my heart, telling me to open it to 1ST. John.

I then saw the Lord's message, as it stood out from the pages of Chapters 4 and 5.

1ST. John 4:4 "You, dear children, are from God and have overcome them, because He who is in you is greater than he who is in the world."

**and**

1ST. John 5:4-5 "This is the victory that has overcome the world, our faith. Who is it that overcomes the world? Only he who believes that Jesus is the Son of God".

"Amen"

# "Gladiator School"

## July 1987

Within days they come to get me. Two Federal United States Marshals arrived at the jail to take me to a United States' Penitentiary

I asked them which prison I was being taken to, and one of them stated that I was being flown to a Federal Penitentiary just outside of Kansas City, Kansas; called "Levenworth".

They then began to cuff me, both at the wrists and at my ankles, and ran chains through the cuffs, finally securing the chains to my waist really tight. It felt like I was an "animal" that they wanted to make sure didn't escape to wreak "havoc" among the people of society.

I had heard stories from convicts at "El-Reno" Prison in Oklahoma; about the "infamous" "Levenworth Federal Penitentiary".

It had a very bad, and extremely "evil" kind of reputation as probably the worst, and most violent Federal prison in "America".

Many convicts called it "The Big House", as it held several thousand convicts, but to the unfortunate men who had called it "home" for many years, it was "The Hot Hour"!

And to everyone who lived there, it was considered "A LIVING HELL"!

I usually don't believe everything that I hear, and only part of what I see, but what I had heard about Levenworth had made the hair on the back of my neck stand up.

As we flew high above the ground, I looked out my window at the clouds below us, and I thought of all of the people out in the "free-world" who were enjoying their lives and loving one another.

I then began thinking about my life, and the past, and of the fact that I am only thirty years old, and no longer free to 'live and laugh and love' along with, and among them.

Only thirty years old, and now with a 40 year 'Federal' prison sentence, along with a 25 years sentence awaiting me back in Florida, that is, if I can survive my Federal prison time without being killed.

My life, in a way, ended at thirty, but in many ways, it had only just begun.

– – – – – – – – – – – – – – – – – –

As we circled around the airport in "Kansas City", preparing to land; I look out the window at the many farms below us, growing their crop of wheat, corn, and soybeans to help feed the world

After landing, and boarding a Federal prison bus, I watched as we passed farm after farm on our way to the prison in Levenworth, Kansas

The fields of wheat looked like they were made of gold, 'sparkling' in the suns' rays as the wind gently swayed the tender stalks back and forth like gentle waves in an ocean breeze

As I laid my head against the bus's window, I thought of the family I was leaving behind and the friends I may never see again, and my eyes began to fill with tears.

"Quickly", I wiped the tears away with the back of my hand, and blinked repeatedly to clear my eyes of wetness, as I had been warned by others that, in prison, crying was considered a sign of weakness, and;

at a place like Levenworth Federal Penitentiary, you don't 'EVER' want to be seen as weak!

It was a 'forty-five' minute ride to the prison, so I listened to the other prisoners, talking about what it was like there, as some had been there before and knew of the bad conditions they had there.

Some of them said that the food was good, but that it was the only good thing about it.

Others talked about the 'violence' and the 'ugliness' that happened there, and what was expected of you there from the staff, and from the other convicts as well.

I kept silent, and listened to what was said as I wanted to prepare myself for what lay ahead of me.

Like on the street, I wanted to create my "own" conditions at Levenworth.

After listening to the other prisons talk about the dangers at Levenworth, I realized that I was about to experience for myself what others already knew, and see "first-hand" why they said it gave them "nightmares".

As we pulled up in front of the prison, my first impression was of a "Gothic Roman Castle", with two large bronze "Eagle" statues staring down at me in front of the building.

The prison building itself was gray, but it's design reminded me of the "White House" in Washington D.C., with a big bronze dome on top.

While "El-Reno", in Oklahoma, was a "medium" security Federal Correctional Institution, "Levenworth" was a "maximum" security level Federal Penitentiary for "hard-core" convicts!

As I looked up at the statues of the two "Eagles", it felt as though their eyes were staring down at me, telling me of the "hardness" of this penitentiary.

It feels like they are telling me that "only the strong survive here"!

I then thought of some American movies I had seen before, and it occurred to me that Levenworth was a "Gladiator School", where you would learn to "fight to the death", or you would die while trying.

For many, many years, "Levenworth Federal Penitentiary" has held the reputation as "the most violent prison in America". It was built to house the "worst of the worst" Federal prisoners that could not be handled at other prisons, the guards told me as I left the bus.

Prisoners that had escaped other prisons were also sent here, as "Levenworth" was by many consideration "escape proof".

To me, it looked like a large "Citadel", and had "fortress like" walls six feet thick surrounding it.

I felt it was a massive "warehouse" of humans, a dirty, imposing and decaying edifice where social conscience rots away, and where "criminality" only gets worse inside these cold gray buildings where hatred grows stronger each day.

Over the years it had become just a stinking "playground" of despicable human perversions, a kind of a monument to the "evil" souls that resided there.

It may seem that my imagination has run away with me, but I can't really even begin to describe the evil that I feel as I walk toward the steps leading into this "God forsaken" place.

As I walked inside, large "ceiling-high" barred doors opened up in front of me, and I carried my property bag through until I was greeted by a group of doctors and nurses who welcomed me with a sack lunch of bologna and cheese, a cookie, an apple and a container of fruit juice.

After lunch I was checked out by the doctors and nurses medically, to make sure I wasn't sick, and they then sent me to a "Lieutenant" at what they called the "Security Inmate System", or "S.I.S".

The "Lt." checked my records to see if I would be staying there, as based on the extreme seriousness of the violence there among the convicts if you were found to be a "snitch", a child molester; or a rapist, the convicts out in the open population would kill you.

They kept all of the new arrivals in building # 23 for two weeks, until they had checked everyone's records to make sure you could stay there.

When I arrived at my temporary cell in Building #23, I found that I was sharing a cell with an old "Colombian Indian".

His hair very long, and went down all the way to his "butt".

He proceeded to answer all of the question I had about "The Big House", as he called Levenworth, and I had many to ask him!

He told me that the "Colombian" people have a community here, and that I would be meeting them shortly.

He spent one week with me, and then told me he would be waiting for me out in open population.

After two weeks I was released from Bldg. # 23 and told to go to my permanent cell housing in Building B-Lower.

I put my property in my locker and locked it up, got my bed made, and after getting everything situated I went out to the recreation yard; where the "Colombian Indian" introduced me to the Colombian community there.

To my surprise I found some of the members of the "Medellin Cocaine Cartel" were there, that I had known before on the outside.

I also met one of the sons of the very infamous "Black Widow", Gryzelda!

In the world of drugs, she is known as the "Black Widow" because of her being very violent and deadly.

She controls her own "drug empire", and will attack you when you least expect it.

You won't even see it coming!

The "Colombian" community welcomed me with large bags of canteen items and groceries, with personal hygiene items and bags of coffee, candies and sweet rolls of all kinds.

They all were warm and shook my hand, wanting to get to know me better; but as soon as I told them that I was a "Christian"; some of them retreated away from me, while some of them who knew me well stayed by me.

It wasn't long after I arrived there that I saw my first "knife-fight" between convicts

One of the guys in our cellblock that worked in maintenance as a painter, was "snitching" on some of the convicts; informing the guards of what they were doing while they smoked some dope in their cells.

Pretty soon two guys come from another building, and went to his cell with "home-made" knives, called "shanks".

They stabbed him repeatedly, over and over, kicked him in the face and groin, and left him for dead, locking the cell door behind them when they left.

When "count-time" come around, his cell-mate found blood all over the floor and walls, and checked him.

Realizing that he was dead, his cellmate told the guard when he come around to count.

The guard just "grinned", then shrugged and said "Well, he shouldn't have been out running his mouth"!

They come with a stretcher and took his bloody body away, carrying it past my cell. He was just a kid really, only 25 years old. He would have been going home in a few months.

After they left with the body they let us out of our cells, and I went into the television room to see what was on. They were all "giggling" about the kid that was murdered in his cell, like it was really funny that he'd bled so much.

I then realized that Levenworth Federal Penitentiary was "just as advertised", and lived up to its tough and very violent reputation, as even the guards turned their backs on murders there.

That night, as I got ready for bed, I told my cellmate that this place is bad.

He then told me that I haven't seen anything yet.

It was almost two in the morning when I was awakened to some strange sounds "echoing" down through our cellblock.

I couldn't make it out at first, but as I lay there on my bunk in my "dark" cell, I could faintly hear cries of pain and anguish and suffering.

I couldn't tell where it was coming from, but the more I listened, the more I could barely make out what was being said.

Someone was crying out in pain, but it sounded like their cries were being muffled by someone else who didn't want them to make any noise to alert the guards.

As I listened, I heard the words:

"You're my boy now, sweetness, and I'm gonna make you love it", which were followed by groans of pain and total humiliation, as a young man was perversely violated again and again by his cellmate.

I felt sick as I realized what was happening and what I was hearing, and I felt like I had to get out of bed and throw up.

As I walked to the bars in front of my cell, my "cell-mate", Robert, spoke to me.

"Sounds like Peter's getting him some tonight"!

"That is so sick and disgusting", I said to Robert as he lit a cigarette. He was doing "triple-life" for killing his whole family!

"I told you, Juan Pablo. You ain't seen nothing yet! This place is like a 'zoo' with predators"!

"Don't the guards hear that"? I asked him.

"Of course they do, but they're not going to do anything about it. Not if they want to stay healthy"! he replied.

"What do you mean by that?" I asked.

"Juan Pablo, this ain't 'El-Reno', this is big bad 'Levenworth', and guards here are stabbed and beaten and killed all the time", he replied.

"Why"? I asked

"Juan Pablo, most of the cons here are total 'psychopaths' who have nothing left to lose, and will kill anyone, including guards; if they are crossed or disrespected in any way"!

"Well", I asked, "don't they separate the young guys away from the sexual perverts and predators?"

"That don't do no good", replied Robert.

"Peter probably paid a guard to move Andrew into his cell with him. It happens all the time here," stated Robert as he made a cup of coffee with warm water from the sink in our cell.

"Paid a guard"? I asked.

"Juan Pablo, you yourself know that people can be 'bought', as you worked in a Colombian Cocaine Cartel that paid people to "look the other way". Guards like money, too, you know"

"I hadn't thought of that," I said to him

"You can even order a 'hit' in here, as there are 'cons' in here who will kill someone for you if you pay them for it," he said to me.

"Robert", I said, "I have asked 'God' to forgive me of my past, which includes what I did while I worked for Pedro Diaz and his "Medellin Cartel"!

"I am determined to live as a 'Christian' man here". I said to him.

"Juan Pablo, 'Christians' are a dime-a-dozen in here, as everyone wants to get released early from prison. It's a 'game' that is played to try to get the parole booed to think you've changed".

"I do not play games with 'God', or my 'faith'", I said sternly to Robert!

"Hey, Bro; calm down! I wasn't saying that you were playing any 'game'! I guess what I should say is that you would be better off here if you stood on your reputation as a Colombian 'Hit-man'!"

"That part of my life is over, and I refuse to live as a 'thug' any longer, Robert".

"Have it your way, Juan Pablo. But don't say that I didn't warn you!" he replied.

I went back to my bunk to lay down again, and heard several 'slaps', and some faint groaning, followed by someone saying "shut-up"! I felt sick inside.

Yes, this place is 'for-real' alright, and was no joke! What I had heard about it was all true.

But, even though it would have been easier to stand on my past reputation as a "killer", I fully intended to stand up for the "Lord"!

As I began to fall back asleep again, I thought of what I had seen happen here already, and of what I had heard people say.

Seeing and hearing all of this made me begin to wonder why men acted this way, and what made them become so mean and violent.

— — — — — — — — — — — — — — — — —

Thinking about it, anyone can go "stir-crazy" from being confined in an '8 x 5' ft. cell for many years at a time, getting more frantic and restless as each day goes by.

The darkness of the cells feel "evil", and smell like mold, and dried blood and "death".

Thinking about the "free-world", but knowing that you may never again be free will drive almost anyone insane.

"Prison life"? It really isn't a "life" at all. It is an "existence" that is highly stressful, and filled with a lot of tension and danger, as you never know if you'll even be alive the next day.

You learn to read "people" just like you read a book, by listening to the tone of their voice, seeing the look in their eyes, and how they stand, or sit. You can tell pretty quickly if they are sincere, or if they're lying to you about something.

Even when you call home on the telephone, and someone says "I Love You", you can tell by the inflection of their voice whether they mean it or not, and if they don't; it tears you apart.

Being "loved" starts meaning "everything" to you, and "birthdays" take on new significance.

"Christmases" in prison are not really a "joyous", cheerful time of year for most prisoners, but a time when they hope and pray that their family and friends will think of them, and maybe send a "Christmas" card; or a letter, or a few dollars for some canteen items they badly need.

To a prisoner, a visit from "family" is worth more than "gold", as it makes them feel "human" again, for a few hours anyway.

A hug and a kiss are "priceless", and quickly brings tears to their eyes.

But most of the men here never have a visit from anyone, family or friends.

Most of them never receive a card or a letter on their birthday, or a loving "Christmas" card or gift.

Most of the men in "Levenworth Federal Penitentiary" were abandoned by their families and loved ones years ago, either because of the crimes they committed, or because they had been locked up so long that it seemed to people on the outside that they no longer existed.

Existing like this in prison makes many men give up all hope, as your "soul" cries out for help and love, but it never comes.

"Love" can heal the broken heart of a man in prison, but not if he never feels any.

After many years behind these walls, a man's heart turns as hard as the gray stone and steel cell that he has to call "home".

— — — — — — — — — — — — — — — — — —

I no longer look back at my past, as I am so ashamed of the evil, violent ways that I acted.

I now only look at today, and what I can do right and good, and of a better future.

I no longer want to hurt people, but want to help in whatever way I can.

I want to be humble, not proud. I want to be wise, and not act like a fool. I want to be free, and not a prisoner to sinful ways.

I want to be a friend, not an enemy. I want to love, instead of hate. I want to build, and not destroy.

I want to be loving, and not violent. I want to heal, and not kill. I want to give, instead of take. I want to forgive, instead of seek revenge.

I want to honor, instead of disrespect. I want to believe, instead of doubt. I want to commend, instead of complain, & I want to be tender, instead of brutal.

My heart cries out for the "forgiveness" and mercy of my fellow man. I hope and pray to "God" that my cries are heard; for how can you live, and strive to better the lives of others, if your heart is empty.

— — — — — — — — — — — — — — — — — —

This morning they found the body of "Mike", one of the men I had met on the recreation yard as I walked the track for exercise daily.

He hung himself last night after the lights were turned off.

He had confided in me, during our daily conversations about never hearing from his family for many years now, and never receiving any help from them

It is so "tragic", as he loved his family so much that he would have taken a "bullet," or a "knife"; for them, and 'died' in their place without even a seconds thought, yet to them he no longer 'existed' anymore.

Mike is the sixth suicide this month at the "Big House", but here, that is quite normal.

— — — — — — — — — — — — — — — — — —

My responsibility here as a Christian is to preach peace, not to watch to see who is doing what to whom, or why.

That is the 'guards' responsibility.

I see things happen, I hear things that are said; but as far as the guards are concerned, I don't 'know' anything.

That is how I have been able to build trust among the gangs in the prison community.

I pray with others here that are seeking "spiritual" guidance.

Sometimes, even though I am only 30 years old, I am asked, 'confidentially', for advice, and have become a counselor to the underworld community here in Levenworth.

One of the gang leaders had ordered a gang member to kill a member of a 'rival' gang. He came to me quietly for advice on what to do. Should he kill him, or not?

I asked him to kneel down and pray with me about it, and let "God" intervene and control the situation, as I believed in the "Lord", and trusted in Him to do the right thing.

"The Lord came through"!

As it happened, they realized that it had been a "misunderstanding", and the killing was called off.

I am so "happy" that I have been able to help arrest a violent, "senseless" killing, but it was the power of "God" that stopped it from happening

Every incoming inmate at "Levenworth" is required to go through an orientation process for one week.

There, the counselor asks you if you've found a job already, or if they need to assign you one:

"Sir, when the dentist checked my teeth, he asked me if I was interested in being a "dental assistant". I told him I would think about it and let him know my decision", I stated to the counselor.

"Well, have you made up your mind yet? The job pays $30.00 per month", he said to me.

"Suddenly," memories from my childhood came flooding back into my mind of wanting to become a doctor and help heal the sick people of the world, and I become "overjoyed" at the prospect of working for a doctor of dentistry; and I loudly, and very happily said

"Yes"!

"I think you've made a good decision. You'll learn a lot from Doctor Smith over in dental". said the counselor.

I went back to my cell from the counselor's office feeling like I was walking on clouds. I hadn't been this happy in many years.

One week later I was assigned a job working for the dentist in his dental office.

On my first day there I was introduced to the leader of the dental clinic, DR. J. J. SMITH.

I found him to not only be an excellent dentist but more importantly, he was a good "Christian" man.

He told me that he would help me in any way he could, and I believed him. He in return wanted me to pay attention, and do my best for him. I happily agreed to this.

He issued me several sets of "medical" white uniforms, so other officers and inmates would know that I worked in the medical dental offices there.

When I put the "white" uniform on, It felt like I was back in the free world again, as Doctor Smith and the nurses treated me like I was a "civilian", instead of an inmate there.

I made sure that I was at work on time every day, always clean and with a pressed white uniform.

I paid close attention to everything he taught me, and always wanted to learn more.

Doctor Smith took notice of my enthusiasm.

Very soon, because of my dedication to my job there, my honesty, my hard work, and my trustworthiness, after about nine months Doctor Smith asked me if I wanted to become a dental technician.

He told me that I would be going to one of the biggest dental laboratories for training, if I accepted the offer.

Very "happily" I said "Yes"!

And within five days I was transferred, and on my way!

# CHAPTER 13
....................................................

## September 9th 1989
# "Gotham City"
# Lewisburg, Pens

I was told that I was being sent to "Lewisburg Federal Penitentiary".

I asked around about "Lewisburg", and I was informed by a lot of people that it was the most dangerous and vicious prison on the east coast of the United States, where even the prison guards were depraved, and would beat you severely if you made them angry for any reason

We were flown to Harrisburg, Pennsylvania from Levenworth, and landed at "Harrisburg", Pen airport, where we boarded a prison bus that took us to "Lewisburg Federal Penitentiary".

As we were coming to within a mile of the prison, I looked up and saw this giant gray building that really gave me the "creeps"!

It looked like a big "castle" that was sitting on top of a mountain!

It reminded me immediately of the castle of the "Count of Monte Cristo"!

As we were approaching the prison, I beg to listen intently to what was being said in the conversations among the other prisoners in the bus that had been there before.

They were talking about the high "body-count" there from killings and suicides.

As the bus pulled to a stop in front of the prison, the officers in the bus started talking about the most recent murder of an inmate!

He was an "electrician" that worked on the inmate maintenance squad at the prison. They said that he had been stabbed in the head with a screwdriver for being a "snitch"!

I asked the officers if this was just a "scare-tactic" that then used to keep the prisoners in line, but they assured me that it was true, and that "Lewisburg" was a very, very violent and dangerous prison.

I then looked out the window of the bus, and in front of me were these huge, "ancient" dark walls surrounding what looked like an old city.

It was so dark and gloomy and dirty, it looked like no one had been taking care of the exterior in a long time.

It reminded me of an abandoned, "lost" civilization.

I then called this place "Gotham City"!

To make it even more "sinister" looking, in the middle of this "city, behind the walls," was a "huge" tower set up high above everything else that had a large "five-point" star mounted on it that was lit up with red light bulbs that glowed "eerily" in the dark!

As the bus waited, a large solid gate opened up, allowing the bus to enter the city.

As the giant gate "slammed" shut behind us with a loud "thud", we stopped in front of an old, dirty and decrepit building.

We were ordered to get off of the bus with our property, and told to walk down some stairs into the basement of the building.

As we went into the basement, we walked through a large wooden door.

As I went inside the room, I noticed several things about it.

Everything was made out of really old, "ancient" looking wood, and I noticed that someone had been polishing the wood on a regular basis, as all of the wood surfaces were smooth and shiny. But, it all looked so old, though, like an "antique".

The second thing that I noticed was the distinctive smell of "human" blood. I am very familiar with that acrid scent, being that I have been working as a dental assistant.

They then put us through the same procedures that I had went through at "Levenworth Federal Penitentiary", with the doctors and nurses, and the case managers and counselors.

There was a difference this time, "though", as I was sent straight into "open-population", as I had already been investigated, and classified.

They assigned me to "C-Block", which was a "maximum security" unit. My cell looked like a closet from the basement of a "dungeon".

After I unpacked my property and put it in my locker, I introduced myself to the guys on my "cell-block", where I met some of the members of the "Christian" community there.

I then met two brothers who had been dubbed "The Golden Boys" in New York City.

They were the "creators" of the "357 Gang," which were heroin distributors in New York.

The brothers told me that they had been praying for "God" to send somebody to help establish a large Christian community there at Lewisburg.

They felt that I was the answer to their prayers because of what I had shared with them about my life, and how God had made me one of "His" children.

In the Colombian community, I was welcomed by two of the sons of the very infamous "Black Widow".

Her youngest son, "Chicky", welcomed me with open arms, as he had known me on the street, out in the "free" world.

They all gathered around me, and they explained to me how things worked in this place, and the "rules and regulations of the underground" here.

I then met people from the different Colombian Cocaine Cartels, some of whom had been my "enemies" before, on the outside.

In prison, they stared at each other like "ravenous" wolves that wanted to attack the other in battle, because out on the street, they would "kill" each other as angry, bitter enemies of each other's "Cartel".

But, that is not done in prison!

In prison, the rules were that you never, ever strike a "fellow Colombian" for any reason.

It was as though there was a truce, or "armistice" in affect while you're incarcerated.

I found that the killings in Lewisburg were happening because of the "infestation" of drugs being brought in from the outside, both by the convicts themselves, and by the prison guards.

What made it easier to kill somebody, was because they had a prison industry that used "fiberglass" to make their products.

It was fairly easy to cut and shape a piece of fiberglass into a sharp knife, with a hard point at the end, and a sharp edge on it. They made both knives, and longer "swords" that way.

It was easy to "smuggle" it out of the industry building, and into your cell-block, because it would be picked up by the metal detectors.

The price of a "well-made" knife made in this way was fifty dollars!

They also had knives in prison they were made of "metal". These were made from left-over pieces of "sheet-metal" that they use to manufacture metal "foot-lockers" for the different military services of the U.S. Government being the Army, Air Force, Navy and Marines. The metal knives also cost you fifty dollars each.

Just about everyone in "Lewisburg" had a knife hidden somewhere, where they could get to it if a situation arose and they needed it!

I felt that I had nothing to fear as long as I walked in obedience to God, as He had promised me that He would protect me from any harm, as one of His children.

But, in other ways I was "scared", and I was "afraid"!

I was "scared" of the many situations that could come up in prisons, where you were "forced" to defend yourself from some violent, uncontrollably "maniac", even if you didn't want to fight anymore

And I was "afraid" that if one of those situations arose, where "calm" reasoning and "Christian" love did not work to stop it, that I might be forced to revert to my former way of dealing with these things, and that my former "thug" mentality would come out, my "killer" instinct would surface, and I would be forced to kill another human being again! This did not want to happen, ever again!

In my past, I was a "highly trained" professional killer who never missed his target.

But my "Lord God" has forgiven me of my past sins, and has given me a "new life" in serving Him, and I never, ever want to harm another human being again. I want to lead them to the "Lord" Jesus. As in Mathew 4:19 b it says:

Mathew 4:19 b "Follow me, and I will make you fishers of men".

October 9, 1989

After one month at "Lewisburg Federal Penitentiary", we were given a tour of the giant "Dental Training Laboratory" there.

We were warmly welcomed by the teacher of the Dental Lab., which were Mr. Earnie Petengill, and Mr. Jimmy Castillo that came from the U.S. Air Force as a dental instructor.

When we started the class the next day, on October 10, 1989; there were twelve of us in the class, which consisted of myself, the two Golden Boys "357"; Michell and Jose Garcia, and nine others.

But, by the time the class graduated four years later, only four of us were left, because of "dexterity" problems.

The four that did graduate were the two "Golden Boys" #357 Michell and Jose Garcia, a Venezuelan named "Ceaser Carlos", and myself.

‒ ‒ ‒ ‒ ‒ ‒ ‒ ‒ ‒ ‒ ‒ ‒ ‒ ‒ ‒ ‒

Within the four years that I was at "Lewisburg", there were many very dangerous and violent incidents where people were both hurt and murdered there for various reasons.

The first me that happened after I arrived there was a murder.

One of the guys that was going home in about three weeks was accused of telling someone that another convict there was "gay", or homosexual

"Jason" was white, and he loved to talk a lot. Whenever he heard someone say anything, whether it was true, or not, about anyone, he just had to repeat it, again and again, until it took on a life of its own.

As it happened, "Jason" had heard a rumor that a "black" convict named "Hanzel" was gay. He walked around to his "buddies" on the recreation yard, and told them what he had heard said about Hanzel.

Word got back to Hanzel that Jason had told everyone he met that Hanzel was "homosexual" and someone's "punk", or lover.

"Hanzel", who at 6'3" tall, 220 lbs. was "furious" at hearing this said about him.

Hanzel was a dead singer for "Michael Jordan", and he also played basketball there at the prison.

And Hanzel, who was always well dressed and nicely groomed, vowed to confront Jason about him spreading this false rumor.

The next afternoon Hanzel came looking for Jason. He found him just as Jason was about to leave his cell to go watch television in the rec. room. Hanzel then confronted him!

"Hey Man"! Hanzel yelled! "What's this I hear about you telling everyone that I'm a homo, and somebody's 'punk'!"

As Hanzel screamed this out loud, it become very quiet in our cell-block, as everyone stopped what they were doing and went out of their cells to see what was happening!

Jason, confronted in front of his cell by Hanzel, tried to back into his cell, but he found that someone was blocking his way.

"Hanzel, I never said anything like that about you", pleaded Jason, as he saw the fiery "hate" in Hanzel's eyes as Hanzel come closer to him.

"Jason's" eyes filled with terror as he saw Hanzel pull out a knife and run towards him, and as he said his last words:

"Hanzel, I never". . . his sentence was cut short as the knife "flashed", quickly plunging into his chest again and again and again, cutting into his heart three times in rapid succession as Hanzel unleashed his heated anger on him in a "murderous" fashion!

Jason then dropped to his knees, a look of total surprise in his eyes, and then fell forward his head bouncing once on the cement floor as it hit, where his life's blood drained out of him, quickly bringing his death!

Everyone parted to one side or the other as Hanzel left.

After that, no one ever said anything about Hanzel, as they didn't want to end up like "Jason"!

I live on the second floor, and this happened on the first floor, directly below me.

Rumors in prison can get people killed. Either by starting a rumor, or spreading one, or being the object of one.

Showing disrespect in this way, or in any other way, is not tolerated in prison, especially in a violent federal penitentiary like "Lewisburg".

If you allow any disrespect to go unanswered when it happens, you are looked upon as being "weak".

You do not ever want to be thought of as weak, as it invites others to take advantage of you, and challenge you "physically", believing that you will not be able to, or even try to stop them from doing so.

- - - - - - - - - - - - - - - - - -

Not long after Hanzel killed Jason, I was out on the soccer field on the recreation yard one afternoon.

As I played soccer among my friends, a Colombian that belonged to another drug cartel walked out onto the recreation yard and watched us play.

This man hated me, and thought that I was hiding behind the Bible there in prison.

Someone kicked the ball to me, putting it in play, and I began to work the soccer ball "down-field" toward our goal line.

As I neared the goal, I sensed someone behind me, and just as I turned my head to see who it was, I received a hard kick behind my right knee!

Grabbing my knee in "excruciating" pain, I dropped to the ground!

As I looked up, I saw that the one who had kicked me was the Colombian from the "rival" drug cartel.

Everyone out on the recreation yard that knew me, both as a "Christian" man, and as the "killer" that I used to be out in the "free"-world were watching me, to see how I would react.

While I was on the ground, I was praying to the Lord, asking for strength to witness in the right way to him in front of the others.

As I got up off the ground, I just simply shook it off and walked away.

Later on, I had the opportunity to talk to him alone, and I shared with him my whole life story.

I told him that I had witnesses in that prison that could testify as to my old ways but that the "Lord had helped me to become a new man, and my old ways were gone forever

I explained to him that that was the reason for me not to react "violently" against him or any other human being for that matter.

He had listened to me for over one and a half hours, and had not interrupted me at all.

He then said to me "I'm impressed, thank you, Juan Pablo"; and walked away.

Later on, he was transferred, and I never did hear from him again.

Yes, there are times when I have a weak moment, and when those moments arise, I pray to the Lord to give me strength to deal with each one of them as he would.

Humans are weak and fallible, and we all need the Lords help on a daily basis to keep walking in his light.

There is so much violence in "Lewisburg" it sickens me.

Everywhere you go here is "dangerous", even the dining hall, what we refer to as the "chow-hall"!

You need to be very careful where you sit down to eat your dinner, as there are certain sections of tables that are claimed by the different gangs here.

If you are not a member of their gang, you do not sit in their section of tables, that is, if you want to go on "living" much longer.

I was at the "chow-hall" on one particular day, and I remember what we had for dinner that evening. It was fried chicken and rice.

After I sat down to eat, I had just taken a bite out of my fried chicken when I was interrupted by a heated conversation a few table over from mine.

One of the members of the "White Knights" gang, a big white convict named "Nino", had walked up to a table, and started talking very loudly at a man that was sitting at that table.

The person sitting at the table was named "Smash".

"Nino" told him, "This table belongs to my "family", and you are not a member of my family, the "White Knight"!"

"Smash" was scheduled to go home in two months but he didn't want to move to another table to eat. At 6'2" tall and 220 lbs. he didn't intimidate easily either

"I said move to another table, you can't sit at my family's table"! yelled "Nino" very loudly, so that everyone in the "chow-hall" could hear him!

"I ain't moving"! stated "Smash", as he stared back hard at "Nino"!

"OH yes you are"! yelled Nino!

"This is a government table and anyone can sit here, so I ain't moving anywhere", yelled Smash!

"We'll see about that"! said Nino, as he left the "chow-hell" for a moment.

"Smash" wasn't paying any attention, as he was continuing to eat his fried chicken off of his tray.

"Nino" walked up behind him and pulled his knife out of his waistband, grabbing "Smash's" head with his left hand, and swinging the knife around with his right hand in an arch, he plunged the knife deep into "Smash's" chest one time!

"Nino" then pulled the knife out of Smash's chest, having punctured his heart with a fatal wound!

"Smash", a look of surprise and terror on his face, got up from his seat and ran towards the back of the "chow-hall", where he dropped to the floor writhing in pain!

Guards called for medical assistance, but "Smash" bled out quickly, and died in a large expanding pool of his own warm blood before any medical assistance could arrive.

"Nino" then dropped his knife under one of the tables and ran out of the "chow-hall", laughing to himself!

It made me feel so sad to see him die like that in front of me, and I cannot believe that someone can be killed simply for sitting at a table and eating their dinner. It made me feel sick inside.

But, the rules of the convicts in a penitentiary are completely different from the rules of the prisons administration.

As a case in point, one day every convict in the prison received a note from the gang leaders

The note stated "Today we are not going to work, and we are not going to eat either. We're "staying down"!"

"If you go against us, we will stab you and burn your cell down"!

Having been here for several years now, and knowing this place well, I knew that that would be exactly what would be done to anybody that went against them.

But, I had made up my mind to live on my knees in front of my God, to be able to stand in front of any man.

No one will force me to go against the principles of my faith and values, even if it costs me my life.

I then prayed, showered, and shaved, then put on my medical whites for work.

When they called "Work call", I walked out of my cell and went to work as usual.

I was joined by Michell and Jose Garcia, and Ceaser Carlos, as I walked down the hall towards the dental clinic.

As we walked toward work, I looked to my left, and to my right, and up against the walls of the cell-blocks I saw many convicts dressed in their jackets, with their arms crossed over their chests.

They were all wearing their boots, which meant that they were "strapped down", armed, and ready to go to "war"!

It was a very dangerous situation, as I knew that the entire prison population could explode into violence at any moment, causing needless death and destruction.

All of the sudden a feeling overwhelmed me, and I sensed a "supreme power" was holding these angry convicts back from attacking us for defying them openly.

I knew that they felt that by us walking past them in the hallway, that we were "challenging" them!

At that moment it felt as though I was walking down the "longest" hallway in the world!

We continued on past them, yet none of them moved toward us.

We realized that we could be killed at any moment, but I knew in my heart that God was in control, and would not let them attack us.

We then went on to the "Dental" Lab. and they took "roll-call" for count.

To my surprise, after "roll-call" they told us to return to our cells, as we were not going to work that day, and were going to be on "lock-down" status.

As everyone entered their cells and were locked down, we could sense and feel the tension in the air, as many of the gang members were very angry that we had defied them opened by going to work today.

What then made matters worse was that I was called by name, and told to report to the "chow-hall" to eat.

Later that night, when it was time for "lock-down" and "lights-out", I knelt down to pray, and it finally "hit" me!

The entire prison population of dangerous angry convicts had been held back by the powerful hand of God, and had been stopped from "rioting"!

"Wow"!

My God is "powerful" indeed!

This was yet another demonstration that "God" is always in control, and only serves to deepen my "faith" in Him!

No one but "God Almighty" could have held back so many angry men!

It never fails to amaze me what "God" can do!

In prison, with so many men confined in close quarters with each other, all it takes is something small and seemingly trivial to set off an "explosion" of violence!

One day, as we came back from work at about three-thirty in the afternoon, there was one of our "Christian brothers" that was watching television.

Everyone called him "Superman"! He was 6'2", and about 200 lbs.

He was enjoying a movie when another convict came into the television room, saw what was playing on the television, and turned to another station without asking if it was ok to switch channels.

The convict that turned the station was named "Spider", and he was 7' tall and weighed about 220 lbs.

"Superman" asked him why he changed the station, as he had been watching that show.

"Spider" took it as a challenge, and ran over to where "Superman" was sitting and attacked him "viciously", throwing him to the floor and kicking him!

They fought "violently" until someone said a guard was coming down to the cell-block!

We were wary of each other, and still quite angry!

I sensed that their altercation that afternoon was not the end of it, and the next morning I was proved correct.

At about six o'clock in the morning, where they pushed a button and unlocked everyone's cell doors, "Superman" was ready!

He knew that early morning was a time when convicts did "surprise" attacks, when you least expected it, and were barely awake

Knowing that, the night before "Superman" had wrapped his body in lots of magazines and newspapers, in case he overslept and wasn't ready to fend off an attack.

### He was right!

"Spider" came running into his cell moments after the cell doors were unlocked, with a long knife in his right hand!

"Superman" saw him coming down the hallway, and jumped up and kicked "Spider" in the chest!

"Spider" doubled over in pain and fell to the floor, the knife falling from his hand!

"Superman" then grabbed the knife off of the floor and jumped on top of "Spider's" stomach, and went into a "frenzy", stabbing Spider over and over and over again, "killing" him!

Many guards came running, but it was too late to save "Spider", who lay in an expanding pool of blood on the floor of "Superman's" cell!

They then locked up "Superman", and transferred him to another penitentiary.

I heard later that he wasn't charged for the killing of "Spider", as it had been deemed a clear case of "self-defense".

— — — — — — — — — — — — — — — — —

As I continued my sentence and dental training at "Lewisburg Federal Penitentiary", I become the leader of the "Christian" community there.

There were many men that were hungry for God's word.

I witnessed to everyone of the power of our "Almighty God", and told of His forgiveness.

I prayed with the convicts wherever and whenever the opportunity presented itself, in their cells, on the yard, in the gymnasium, at the education building, and in the chapel!

"Everywhere"!

Many of these hardened convicts accepted the oration.

The Lord works in many ways, and sometimes He'll even give you a "test".

This one evening, as I was walking around the recreation yard, one of my friends came up to me and told me that there was someone looking for me from the "chow-hall".

I asked my friend, "Who is it?"

He said "I don't know, it's a new guy that just arrived here a few days ago, Juan Pablo".

I went over to the "chow-hall", and there he was, standing in front of me, one of the men that had testified against me at trial!

He had testified at both my Federal trial, and again at my murder trial in Miami.

As I walked up to him in the "dining-hall", he was holding his food tray with both hands, and shaking like a leaf!

His tray held the pork chops and rice that we were having for supper that night.

He looked really "pale", and the color had drained out of his face.

As he looked up and saw me walking towards him, he jumped; almost dropping his tray of food.

He had absolute "terror" in his eyes as I got nearer to where he was standing, and the first statement out of his mouth was:

"J-J-JUAN PABLO, I H-H-HEAR THAT YOU ARE A C-C-CHRISTIAN NOW"!

With a very calm voice; I replied:

"Yes, I am a Christian now. One hundred percent!"

He relaxed a little, and began to eat his dinner with a look of amazement on his face, the color returning to his cheeks again.

I smiled and sat down next to him after I received my food tray, and we ate dinner together for the first time in many years.

I took this meeting with him again in my life as a test from God, because, as the rules and regulations of the Federal Government state, "co-defendants" are not supposed to be in the same prison camp together, if they have testified against each other at trial.

I was very glad, and amazed, that I felt no hate or bitterness or anger, or any animosity towards him.

I only felt a sense of "Christian" love and understanding towards him now, as I knew that God was using him as a "tool" to fulfill in my life His plan for me.

I shared with him my clothes, sweatshirts, pants, shoes and sox, as he had none, and we both wore about the same size anyway.

I gave him a bag of canteen goodies, as he had no money of his own to purchase any.

Then, I introduced him to "Jesus Christ", the Savior of my "soul"!

He started going to church with me in the "chapel" regularly, and reading his Bible that I gave to him.

I caught him looking at me several times with an "amazed" expression on his face, like he was really looking at a new man.

I found out that he was telling others there about my past life on the outside, and of my job as a "contract killer" for the "Medellin Cocaine Cartel" that was operated by "Pedro Diaz" in "Colombia".

He told many of them about how dangerous and violent I used to be, and of the "Christian" man that I have become, and of how he saw that these were two totally different people.

When I asked my counselor why he was gone, he told me that he had been mistakenly sent there, and had to be moved because he had testified against me.

Two months later one of my countryman got into an altercation with another convict, who happened to be a member of one of the many gangs there at the prison, stabbing him several times.

Being that it was a member of a "Porto Rican" gang that was stabbed, their gang-leader sent a message to the leader of the "Colombian" gang.

"We declare war on you, and the "battlefield" will be the gymnasium"!

This meant that they will strike any "Colombian", whether he is a member of the Colombian gang, or not!

The attack was set for six o'clock the next evening.

The "Porto Rican" gang had members in all of the "quads", just as the "Colombian" gang had members in all of the cell-blocks.

The "Porto-Rican" gang was to attack the "Colombians" in the cell-blocks simultaneously at the same time as the attack in the gymnasium started.

The plan was to stuff paper and debris into the keyhole of the door leading into the gymnasium after the guard locked us in at 6:00 pm, which would prevent the officers from unlocking the door and getting back in once the battle started.

When I found out about this, I went to my cell and knelt down on my knees, and cried out to the "Lord" for help!

"Please Lord", I cried, "Please stop the war before it gets started"!

"Amen"!

One of the guys in the "cell-block" come to me, and told me that the "Colombian" gang were going to have a meeting downstairs in five minutes

I had never been to one of their meeting as I am not a member of any gang, but I chose to attend this meeting.

The leader of the Colombian gang addressed the Colombian community with the following statement:

"We are going to have a 'war' with the "Porto-Rican" gang, and I want everyone of you to grab your knives and go to the gymnasium at 6:00 pm!

"Well, don't count on me to help your kill"! I stated; after he had finished addressing the members. "I see 'their' blood in the same way as I see 'your' blood, and besides that, I fight all of my battles from my knees"!

The leader of the "Colombian" gang then turned to me and stated:

"Ok Juan Pablo, let's see when they come at you with their knives whether your 'Bible' can stop the knife from piercing your heart"!

"When something happens to you, Juan Pablo, don't call on us to help you!" he said aloud.

"You know that I am not a member of your gang", I said to the leader.

"The only reason I came to this meeting was because I was told that what is going to happen will concern all' Colombians, not just gang members! Otherwise, I would not be here"

Later on that afternoon I heard the good news!

The "Porto-Rican" gang that was going to attack the Colombians had held a meeting among themselves.

In the meeting, one of the "gang leaders" made the following statement to all of the members.

"If anybody touches Juan Pablo, or any of the Colombians that are in church then the fight is going to be among us, with ourselves!"

He made that statement because he knew me very well. He knew that I was a real "Christian" that practices what I preach, as I don't just "talk the talk", I "walk the walk"!

He had heard what I had said to the Colombian gang leader, at 'their' meeting.

Then, the "Miracle" took place!

The "Porto-Rican" gang leaders agreed among themselves that the Porto-Rican gang member had disrespected the Colombian by what he had done, and he had deserved what he got.

They then declared that the "Colombian — Porto-Rican" war was off!

Once again, the "Lord" had heard my prayers!

# CHAPTER 14

## "Dodge City"
### 1993

Atlanta, Georgia

After finishing my "dental technology" training, and graduating my class, I was then transferred to Atlanta Federal Prison in Atlanta, Georgia.

It immediately struck me just how large a prison it was. As I looked around at all of the buildings that comprised the prison's compound I took notice of how old that most of the buildings were.

Asking around, I found out that many of the prison's buildings were more than a hundred years old, and had been built with slave labor. It kind of rattled me when I was told that the prison actually was built on top of an old cemetery that had hundreds of bodies still in their graves. I felt that it had been wrong to do this, as it "desecrated" many people's final resting places.

As I talked to one of the prison's guards I was told that Atlanta Federal Prison is the largest Federal Prison in American, and the it held over 2500 convicts.

After they finished processing me through medical and classification, they sent me to "open population" where I was assigned to my permanent cell-block.

As I looked around the "cell-block" I would be calling home, I saw how utterly filthy and decrepit this prison was. It smelled "rotten"!

As I entered my cell, I noticed the acidic smells of urine, sweat, and human blood. It made me sick to my stomach, and I felt like I was going to be sick, and vomit at any moment.

The cell was "filthy", and had green mold all over the walls and ceiling where the pain was literally hanging down in large pieces, ready to fell to the floor, or onto your head.

As I unpacked my property to put it away in my locker, I jumped back suddenly, surprised by a large family of cockroaches that came running out of my footlocker, scattering in every direction. I found out why they were there, as I found a dead mouse underneath some old newspaper in the corner of the locker, which smelled very badly.

Seeing me jump back, some of the other convict on my "cell-block" busted out laughing, saying that I was evicting the regular tenants of the cell, so that I could move into their house.

As I inspected my mattress to make my bed up, I found that it was filled with hole where the stuffing was falling out of it everywhere

I knew that I wouldn't be able to find another mattress before lunch, so I went ahead and made my bed up, covering the holes as best as I could.

I had thought that the other prisons I had been at were bad, but I was in for a very awakening, as this place was, as they say in the old time chain-gang, "off the chain"!

As I entered the "chow-hall," I saw flies on the tables and roaches all over floor, eating the crumbs of food that had been dropped off of the food trays.

I got in line to get a tray, as we were having hamburgers, but as I picked up my tray, I saw that it had a few slices of bologna and some bread instead. I asked the man next to me if they had somehow ran out of hamburger meal and he "laughed," saying that that was not the case.

"Bro, you must be new here", he said to me.

"I am, I just arrived this morning", I replied.

"No, they didn't run out of hamburger they never bought any for us to eat", he stated matter of fatly.

"Why not"? I asked him.

"Because the staff here at Atlanta Federal Penitentiary is very corrupt", he stated.

"Has anybody filed a lawsuit about it"? I asked him.

"Nope, and no one is going to either", he said.

"Why not,? The prisoners food is paid for by the Federal Government"?

"Because, dude, no one wants to get the "hell" beat out of them by either the guards, or the convicts, that's why"!

"Why would they get beaten by the guards or other convicts"? I asked him

"We'd better eat now, I'll explain what's going on when I see you out on the recreation yard after lunch", he stated.

I finished my bologna sandwich and was returning my empty food tray to the dish room when I heard yelling at a table behind me.

"Don't you ever reach over my food again you idiot", yelled one convict to another, as he swung his fist and hit him in the mouth!

After getting up off of the floor, the one that had been punched reached over and picked up his fork, ran over to the man that had hit him, and plunged the fork deep into his right eye, twisting it "savagely" before pulling it back out, taking the eyeball out of its socket!

Letting out a "blood-curdling" scream, the inmate ran blindly in pain and terror, slamming into the wall of the "chow-hall" as he ran!

I looked on in "horror" as this unfolded in front of me, wondering what had brought on this violent fight, yet I didn't know who to ask.

As I walked back to my "cell-block" before recreation yard call, I asked one of the convicts next to me what caused the fight.

"It doesn't take much to start a fight here, 'bro'"! he said to me.

"Do you mean that just for reaching for the salt and pepper you can get stabbed or killed"? I asked him.

"Yep, if your arm, hand or elbow crosses over someone's food tray"! he replied.

I just shook my head sadly, as I had hoped that "Atlanta Federal Penitentiary" would not be as violent as Levenworth or Lewisburg had been.

As I got ready to go to the recreation yard, I was introduced to some of the members of the "Christian" community there. I was informed that they had been praying hard for some kind of positive change to take place here, as it was just too "wild", even for a Federal Maximum Security Prison. I then prayed with them on this.

When I went out onto the recreation yard, I was met by "J. J.", when I had met in the chow hall when we had received bologna instead of hamburger meat.

"Now we can talk", he said, as he walked up to me, offering his hand.

"My name is 'Juan Pablo'", I said, as I shook his hand.

"People call me "J. J"., glad to meet you, Juan Pablo".

"You were saying that the staff here is corrupt", I said, as I sat down on a concrete bench.

"Yes, it is very corrupt, in a lot of ways, but we can't really do anything about it here without starting a riot or something," he stated matter-of-factly.

"Why is that"? I asked him.

"Well, where do I begin"? he said, as he sat down next to me on the bench.

As I listened, he began to explain to me how things worked here.

"Juan Pablo", he said. "In many ways we have to just go along with how they run things here to keep things running smoothly."

"Why is that"? I asked him.

"Well, take our visits with our wives or girlfriends for instance. If we want to 'make love' to them, we just pay a guard one hundred dollars to look the other way for awhile, and we can spend some time in the sack with them". he said.

"The guards take bribes"? I asked him.

"OH Yes, they'll even wink at you when you're done, and ask both of you if you've enjoyed yourselves".

"Is that the extent of the corruption"?

"OH, No". He stated.

"What else"?

"Juan Pablo, you can get just about anything brought in to this prison, if you have money".

"Like what"? I asked him.

"Drugs for one thing, pornography is another, and just about any kind of property you can think of that you'd want."

"Property?

"Yes"!

"What kind of property are you talking about"?

"Well, let's see. Watches of any kind, radios, cell-phones, clothes, shoes and boots, rings, any kind of hygiene items. Just whatever you want to get you can have brought in, if you pay the guards enough"!

"And they get away with it"? I asked him.

"Who's to stop them, another crooked prison guard"? he replied.

"To tell you the truth, none of this really surprises me". I said to him.

"Didn't they do the same at the other places you've been at"?

"Not to this extent", I said to him.

"So you can see now why we can't really try to change things around here. The guys here care more about what they can get than they do about a piece of 'hamburger' meat on their food tray"!

"Yes, I can see your point, 'J. J'.".

"And, if someone was to be dumb enough to report any of this to the authorities, they wouldn't live very long in here". he said to me.

"I can understand that". I replied.

"This place is 'weird' in a lot of ways", he stated.

"What do you mean, 'weird'"? I asked him.

"Well, they've got a whole bunch of 'Jamaican's here that practice 'Voodoo'"!

"VOODOO"! I repeated loudly!

"Yes, Juan Pablo. 'Voodoo'"!

"J. J., Voodoo is an 'African' cult worshiping rite that uses chicken blood in the ceremony"! I stated to him.

"Juan Pablo, here they use the blood from dogs that they kill, especially young 'puppies'"!

"WHAT"!? I screamed!

"Yes, you heard me right, puppies"!

"This is unbelievable"! I yelled, as I stared hard at 'J. J'!

"I know that you've noticed the dogs running around out here since you've arrived, Juan Pablo. I wouldn't get too attached to any of them". he stated flatly to me.

I love dogs, especially "puppies", and the thought of some idiot purposely killing one and using it's blood in a 'cult' ceremony made me feel sick, and very very "angry"!

"There must be something we can do to stop that from happening, 'J. J.'". I said to him, as I shook angrily, my temper beginning to flair!

"Calm down, Juan Pablo! There is nothing you can do about it without getting yourself hurt, and probably killed! They'd burn your cell up with you in it"!

"But to do that to 'puppies' that can't defend themselves is monstrous"! I screamed loudly!

"I know, Juan Pablo, but those idiots believe in that 'cult' garbage"! he stated as he shrugged his shoulders.

"I'll tell you one thing 'J. J.', They'd better not ever let me catch one of them doing it, as it will take "God" Himself to pull me off of them"! I said "angrily"!

"As I told you before Juan Pablo, this prison is very very wild and violent. There are fights and stabbings almost every day here."

"Why so much of it"? I asked him.

"There's many reasons for it, Juan Pablo. People have nothing to look forward to in here. Most of their families have abandoned them on the outside and never write to them, or send them cards, or even a care package at "Christmas", or anything that shows that they care about them anymore. The majority of guys in here have just given up on life."

"What about the 'Christian' community. Don't they invite others to the "Chapel" services"?

"Yes, we do invite them to come to the chapel with us for services, but most of the time someone else will step to them and ask them if they want to smoke some 'dope', or drink some homemade 'wine', and they end up skipping out on coming to the chapel."

How big is the "Christian" community here"? I asked him.

"Taking into account that there's 2500 convicts here, not that big, Juan Pablo"!

"Why not"? I asked him.

"Well, it's not that they don't come to the chapel, Juan Pablo, it's that they hardly ever come back a second time". he replied.

"Why"? I asked him.

"They're just not that interested, Juan Pablo".

"Don't they ever have any 'special' religious programs with guest speakers"? I asked him.

"Maybe once or twice a year someone will come and sing some songs, or something, but I wouldn't really call it 'special', Juan Pablo".

"At Levenworth we called the prison 'The Big House', and sometimes 'Hell House'.

What do you call this place"? I asked.

"Dodge City"! He stated with a straight face.

"Why 'Dodge City'"? I asked.

"Because of everything that goes on here. The violent attacks, the rapes, thefts, pretty much everything, Juan Pablo. It's like a town in the

"Wild Wild West" where it's wide open and "untamed," with no law and order, and a town Marshall that's ineffective at keeping the peace"!

— — — — — — — — — — — — — — — — — —

Later on that night I was reading my Bible when I heard 'screaming' from the other end of the cell-block!

"What's going on"? I asked the guy in the cell next to mine.

"Someone threw a torch cocktail into Charly's cell with 'him' in it"!

"Why did they do that?" I asked him.

"They said that 'Charly' snitched on them for smoking some 'dope' last night"! he replied.

I watching as the medical help arrived, and found out that it was too late, as Charly was already dead in his cell!

"I've went from bad to worse"! I thought to myself, as they locked our cell doors, putting our cell-block on "lock-down" status!

— — — — — — — — — — — — — — — — — —

I watched as he took his first steps, all by "himself"! He looked down at his new shoes and giggled, slowly putting one tiny foot out in front of him as he tried to keep his balance without falling. He looked up at me and grinned as he took another 'shaky' step, coming closer and closer with each one.

I held out my arms as he came closer, so very proud of him. As he got to within three feet of me, he raised his little arms up and, putting on an unexpected burst of speed, ran straight into my arms!

"Da-Da"! He said, as he reached his little hand up and grabbed my nose, squeezing it with strength that belied his tiny size.

"Daddy loves you"! I said to him as I held him in my arms, gently hugging my "precious" little son as tears of joy and happiness rolled down my cheeks.

"Love Da-Da"! he said, as he hugged me back, bringing a smile from his mother sitting next to me, my wonderful wife that I love so very much!

—  —  —  —  —  —  —  —  —  —  —  —  —  —  —  —

As my eyelids blinked open, the smile on my face disappeared as my eyes focused on the large flakes of paint ready to fall from the gray ceiling, and the bars in the door of my cell.

I reached up and touched my cheeks, and my fingers felt the wetness of tears.

But, they were tears of "happiness", as I know that my "Lord" gave me this dream to reaffirm His promise to me that I will one day be free to do His will in my life.

And I know that "God" does not lie!

"Thank you, Lord"! I said out loud, as I got up to dress for breakfast.

As I knelt down to pray, I asked my "Lord" to watch over my family on the outside, and keep them healthy and happy, and away from all that would harm them.

I asked that He would keep an eye on me also, as I am in a very violent, mean and dangerous place. But, I put my faith and trust in "Him" to show me how to deal with each situation that may come up, so that I may do "His" will, and not my own.

After breakfast I was introduced to members of the "Colombian" community here in Atlanta Federal Penitentiary.

I was surprised at how many of them I knew from "Colombia", and even Miami!

One of them, "Anibal" was an enemy from Miami that I had taken a "contract" to kill in 1982, but had been unable to locate.

When "Anibal" found out that I was there, he told several members of the "Colombian" community that I still held a "contract" on him.

I was then approached by one of the "Colombians" from the Christian community, who asked me if I intended to "fulfill the contract"!

With a smile on my face, and tears in my eyes, I said to him:

"Please tell 'Anibal' that I no longer work for Mr. 'Pedro Diaz', or the 'Medellin Cartel', and that I do not hold a 'contract' on him".

"I now work for someone 'infinitely' more powerful, my 'Lord God' in Heaven, and do only what is 'His' will for me in my life"!

"Tell Anibal that 'God' holds the contract on 'my' life"!

With a hug and a smile, the 'Colombian' walked away and relayed my message to a very nervous "Anibal", who broke down in tears.

He had been so "fearful", and afraid that he would be found by me, and killed!

I realized then that it may take many years to live down my past reputation as a "hit-man", but I will have to do it one day at a time.

I then met Anibal at the chapel, and was very pleasantly surprised to find out that he also was now a "Christian", and had thrown away his past, and was a child of "God"!

He has a "wonderful" singing voice, and is a member of the choir here. His favorite hymn is "Amazing Grace".

Several months after arriving here I was walking on the track on the recreation yard when a friend from the chapel ran up to me!

"Juan Pablo, did you hear about Tommy"?

Tommy was a dear friend that I had met at the chapel, who had been having problems with his wife. She had asked for a divorce, since Tommy had a twenty year sentence, and she didn't want to wait that long for him to get out of prison. He had loved her with all of his heart.

"No, I haven't heard anything! What is the matter"? I asked him.

"He cut his wrists last night! They just found him in his cell! He's dead, Juan Pablo"!

"OH, My God"! I cried, as tears come to my eyes. He had given up on "life"!

I had been praying with him about this, and told him to put it in God's hands.

But it seems that "Satan" had been talking to him, and he had listened to him instead.

I felt very bad for over a month after Tommy's death. His suicide reminded me of how weak we are as "humans", and of how much we need to put our faith in "God" with all of our troubles.

Nine months in "Atlanta Federal Penitentiary" seemed like nine years, and I began praying for a transfer away from here.

One night, as I was getting ready to take my shower, I heard yelling coming from the shower room!

As I stepped out into the hall, I saw one of the young convicts running out of the shower room with a knife in his hand!

He was covered with blood as he ran down the hall and into his cell!

Several people looked into the shower, and found that the kid had stabbed a guy named "Lucky Eddie" about ten times, and he was laying in a large, spreading pool of blood!

I watched as "Lucky Eddie" looked up at us and smiled. Then, as he coughed up a mouthful of blood, he spoke his last word, "Sweet", before his eyes rolled back in his head and he went limp, dying with his eyes open!

He had been called "Lucky Eddie" because he was a "homosexual rapist", and had been in Atlanta Federal Penitentiary for ten years and had not been killed by anyone yet.

"Lucky Eddie's" luck had finally ran out, as he had met, and victimized, someone who had fought back. The young convict that he had raped in the shower was not charged for his death, as it was deemed self-defense.

I began to work hard to expand the Christian community inside Atlanta Federal Penitentiary, and I prayed with the inmates daily.

As I shared my testimony with many of these men, they came to realize that the power of "God" is immense, and that prison is not the "one way street to Hell" that they had thought of it as.

There will always be temptations from "Satan", as our Lord tells us that "Satan" has dominion over the earth.

But, that does not mean that we have to listen to what Satan tells us, or that we need to follow his examples.

Change comes from "within", and with one "Lord" in our hearts, we can resist what Satan tells us, and can walk with God as His children.

After fourteen months at Atlanta Federal Penitentiary, I was overjoyed when the Lord answered my prayers, and I was transferred to Allenwood Federal Penitentiary, in Allenwood Pennsylvania on February 20th, 1994.

# CHAPTER 15

## "All The King's Men"
### Feb. 1994

Allenwood, Penn.

I arrived at "Allenwood Federal Penitentiary" on February 28th, 1994. As we pulled up to the front of the prison, I noticed that many of the convicts that were in the bus with me were starting to get nervous.

I asked one of them why they were acting scared, and he told me that the guards at Allenwood don't play, and were really mean to the new arrivals.

As we were brought in for processing through property & classification, and given medical evaluations I sat my bags of property down on the floor, as they were getting a bit heavy from carrying them with me everywhere I went.

I began searching for a restroom as it had been hours since we had boarded the bus for transport.

After I returned to the group, one of the prison guards began yelling at all of us to strip down to our boxer shorts and T-shirts. After everyone had complied, he ordered us to dump our personal belongings out of the bags and boxes, and onto the floor.

He then walked in front of all of us, and using his boots, kicked our personal belongings across the concrete floor, making a big mess, and mixing everyone's property together.

After doing this, he turned back toward us, sneered, and said; "anyone have something to say about that"?

We just looked at the floor, as none of us were foolish enough to challenge him for doing it, which would become a one-way ticket to "solitary confinement".

After our "strip-search", we got dressed again and went through medical, where the doctors and nurses checked us for any kind of diseases that we may have, and took some blood samples from all of us.

In the classification department, they assigned me as a staff cook, which meant that I would be preparing food for the staff, including the "Warden" of the prison.

That also meant that I would be able to eat better food, as the staff almost always eats higher quality food than the prison convicts do.

After being assigned to my permanent cell-block, I introduced myself, seeking out the members of the "Christian" community there

As I soon found out to my dismay, it barely existed there at Allenwood Federal Penitentiary.

I began in earnest to change that, and after meeting the Chaplain, I started inviting everyone I could to the "Chapel" services, and started prayer groups, both for English and Spanish language convicts.

The men here were hungry for God's word, and soon we had a large "Christian" community at Allenwood!

Things were going ok for awhile, but then things began to get more violent as many new convicts were transferred in.

After I had been at Allenwood Federal Penitentiary for almost a year, a young man come to Allenwood, and he joined the "Christian" community. His name was "Jonathan".

Several days later, a leader of one of the many gangs here, the "King's Men", approached me, and told me:

"I want you to close the doors to the church to 'Jonathan', and not allow him to come to church with your group".

"Why," I asked him?

"He is an enemy of ours from the streets, and his gang has a beef with ours"!

I then said to him:

"The church is not my church, it belongs to our Lord Jesus Christ, and I cannot close the doors to anyone".

"If he is a real 'Christian', I am going to stand behind my brother in Christ".

He then said:

"So, you are against us"?

I said:

"No, I always respect you, and others, but this time I have to respectfully deny your request"!

"We shall see about that", he then said as he walked away angry.

From his actions I felt that there may be trouble brewing, and I was right.

The next day, as I was coming back to my unit at 1 PM from work, someone called out to me, and as I looked back, I saw someone running towards me. I stopped and waited for him.

"Juan Pablo", he said; "the 'Kings' had a meeting today, and I heard them say what they're going to do to you"!

"What is that"? I asked him.

"They said that they were going to stab you, and then burn you to death in your cell, and everything in it"! he said to me.

"Thank you for telling me", I said to him, and went directly to my cell. It is a "two man" cell, with only me in it right now.

Once inside my cell, I knelt down on my knees and called out to my "Lord Jesus"!

"Lord, I claim your promise of 'Exodus', Chapter 14; verse 14";

"Stand still, for the battle is mine".

I decided that I am not going to hide myself from anyone, or ask for protection, and I don't want to share this with anyone but my "Lord".

Later that day they called out the 4 PM canteen run.

One of the members of the "King's Men" jumped to the front of the line in front of everyone else, and got in front of a member of a "Mexican" gang.

The "Mexican" gang member then smashed the "King's Men" gang members face and head into a concrete wall!

As soon as that happened, they very quickly put the whole prison on "lock down".

Within about two hours the "lock-down" was lifted, and the prison resumed normal operations again.

Once again, a "miracle" had happened, and the "Lord" answered my prayer.

They had transferred all of the "King's Men" out of the prison, and sent them to other institutions while we were locked down. There was not even one left there at Allenwood.

I learned that "God" will become real to the people that are real with Him!

On the following Saturday morning, during breakfast a convict was sitting next to me at my table. We were eating cinnamon rolls, cereal and milk.

I didn't know him, so I said "Hello, I'm Juan Pablo".

That was the "ice-breaker"

He then began sharing with me the good news that he had won the appeal on his case, and that within two months he would be released from prison.

I saw the perfect opportunity to share with him the "plan of salvation"!

I thought that I did a really good job of presenting God's plan of salvation to him that day.

My main concern is, that if you leave prison without "Christ" in your heart, you will not make it on the outside.

When I finished talking to him, he said:

"Thank you, Juan Pablo, but I am too young for religion, and I need to get back to 'taking care of business' when I get out of prison, and I have no time for that 'religious stuff' that you are talking about".

The next morning, as I was going to the "Chapel", his cell-mate, whom I had known for years, said:

"Juan Pablo, you're not going to believe this"!

I said, "What's up"?

He said, "Every morning, after I get up, I grab our coffee cups and go get us some hot water for our coffee, my cell-mate and me".

"Yes, I know", I replied.

"Well, this morning when I tried to wake him up, he didn't answer".

"Then, when I touched him, and tried to wake him up, he was ice-cold"!

"He's dead, Juan Pablo"!

"How old was he"? I asked.

"He was thirty-four years old"!

"What happened?" I asked him.

"Well, last night he was 'celebrating' the good news of going home, and he got a hit of 'heroin'. He overdosed, Juan Pablo"!

I realized at that moment that, since he had died without accepting Jesus as his Lord and Savior, that he had sent himself directly to Hell! It was too late for him, now.

Two weeks after that happening, I was talking with one of the men that worked with me in staff dining. His name was "Alonso".

I gave him the same message of "salvation".

He then said to me:

"Juan Pablo, I'm the devil himself! Please don't preach to me, ok"!

From then on, every time I told him that I would pray for him, he would say:

"I don't believe in that garbage, Juan Pablo, and remember, I'm the 'devil' himself"!

One morning not long after that, as I was getting ready for breakfast, I looked outside of my cell door at six AM.

Suddenly, Alonso's door is wide open, and then 'Alonso', with a face so "white" it looked like he'd seen a ghost, come out of his cell, and walked towards me. He was totally terrified!

I thought that something bad had happened to him!

He then started crying, and said:

"Juan Pablo, I need your help"!

"Why, what happened?" I asked him.

He then said:

"This morning, at about 3 AM, a voice wake me up and told me that I need to change my life, or I'm not going to make it"! He then said:

"Juan Pablo, what do I need to do to become a Christian?"

We knelt down together on our knees, and I asked him to repeat after me as we said the sinner's prayer; the prayer of repentance.

After we finished praying, he hugged me and smiled broadly.

"Thank you, Juan Pablo". He said, as he walked away, looking like a huge weight had been lifted from his shoulders.

He was released soon after that, and married a nice Christian woman he had met at church.

She owned a restaurant, and now he is the cook there.

Their restaurant business is doing great, and his marriage is wonderful!

By putting the "Lord" first and foremost in his life, and trusting in Him completely, he has totally turned his life around, and is an outstanding members of his community.

He no longer drinks, or uses any drugs and is a volunteer in many community outreach activities.

He wrote me a letter recently, and sent pictures of himself and his wife, and the restaurant they own, thanking me, and telling me of all the blessings he has received from the Lord.

# CHAPTER 16

## "The Valley Of Death"
### April 3, 1997

Lompoc, California

After a little more than three years at Allenwood, I was transferred to "Lompoc Federal Penitentiary" in Central California, which is located about three hours north of "Los Angeles".

I arrived on April 3, 1997; and went through the usual processing; medical, dental, psychological and classification departments.

On my first afternoon there, I went to the "chow-cell" at dinnertime, and sat down at a table to eat my food, which was roast beef and potatoes.

After finishing my plate, I was sitting there eating my orange that was the "dessert" we had that meal.

As I was peeling my orange at about 5 PM, an inmate came running in to the "chow-hall"!

He had a "wild" look in his eyes as he ran, and I then noticed that he had two knives, one tied to each of his hands!

He looked around the "chow-hall" for a brief moment, then, running as fast as he could, he "lunged" at a group of four prison guards that were standing there talking!

As I looked on, and before anyone could stop him, he began stabbing all of the guards in the chest area repeatedly!

There was so much blood pouring out onto the floor, and onto the guard's hands, that it made it very difficult to stop the inmate from his deadly attack, and subdue him.

Finally, after what seemed like an eternity, but was in fact only a few moments, other prison guards arrived on the scene and tackled the inmate, 'wrestling' him to the floor!

As he was put into a "headlock", and handcuffed, he began screaming at the top of his lungs, saying:

"Kill me, kill me, I want to die"!

I had no doubt in my mind that the prison guards wanted to give him his wish at that moment!

As they took him away, the nurses and a doctor from the medical department arrived, and began to check and treat the injured guards that were laying on the floor in an expanding pool of blood!

One of the guards, "Scott Williams", wasn't responding, and died of his injuries before an ambulance could get him to the hospital.

Of the other three guards, one went into a "coma" from the loss of most of his blood from fourteen stab wounds, and the other two guards were in critical condition in the hospital.

Several of the convicts there later told me that the inmate that attacked the guards was a "paranoid schizophrenic" that way not being treated with medication that he needed.

That, on my first day there, was my introduction to "Lompoc Federal Penitentiary".

Of the six years I spent at "Lompoc Federal Penitentiary", the first three years were the worst, and they were very "eye opening" to say the least.

I found "Lompoc" to be comparable to "Levenworth Federal Penitentiary", as far as both the level of violence, the murders of the inmates, and of the staff corruption.

But, "Lompoc" topped the list as far as the suicide rate of the inmates there, and the incidents of convicts killing other convicts, sometimes for no apparent reason.

Within my first week at "Lompoc" there were two suicides and one murder.

I asked around, and found out that the main reasons for the suicides were abandonment by family and loved ones, and because of wives filing for divorce from their husband that had either a long prison sentence, or a "life" sentence.

Both of the suicides that took place shortly after my arrival were done with overdoses of heroin taken on purpose.

One of the men that killed himself "Allen", was despondent over his family that no longer came to visit, or even bothered to write to him anymore.

In waiting to use the telephone, I had witnessed him try time after time to get someone on the phone to accept a call, but all of them were refused. It seemed that no one cared about him anymore, couldn't forgive him, and would show him no mercy.

The second suicide was "Jerry". His wife had written him a "Dear-John" letter, telling him she had met another man, and was divorcing him to get remarried.

He couldn't handle losing both her, and his five year old daughter, "Cynthia".

The drug overdoses were a common occurrence at "Lompoc", as heroin was very easy to get there.

It was both smuggled in by inmates coming back from "visitation", and brought into the prison by crooked prison guards and sold to the convicts. It was as easy to get as buying a soda pop, or a candy bar.

The murder that took place soon after I got there was senseless.

Two convicts, each belonging to a different prison gang, were walking down a hallway, and bumped into each other.

Both of them accused the other of being at fault, and neither one would apologize to the other.

At first they got into a shaving match, which escalated into a "fist-fight", which then ultimately ended with someone throwing one of them a "shank", or homemade knife, which was used to stab one of them a half a dozen times until he dropped to the floor, coughed up blood, and died in a pool of blood.

Other murders were brought on by an inmate "snitching", or informing the guards of someone's illegal activities, usually to either gain favor with the guards, or to get some extra privileges.

Rapes of younger inmates by hardened convicts were commonplace at "Lompoc", and it seemed to me that the guards there turned a blind eye towards it's occurrence.

Usually it was a young "slightly" built inmate that was intimidated by an older, "larger", hardened convict with a long sentence and a history of sexual violence toward others.

They would either pay a guard to have the weaker inmate moved into their cell, or they would attack him in his own cell when he was alone, threatening him with harm, or even death, if he told anyone about what happened.

Sometimes the victim would try to fight back to protect himself during the assault. That usually ended up with the victim being beaten badly, and sometimes killed.

Most of the time, the prison guards at "Lompoc Federal Penitentiary" didn't do their regular rounds, which includes walking around in the cell-blocks and checking inside the individual cells. It was well known to the prison population that the guards were lazy, and activities such as using drugs were planned accordingly.

Supervision of the inmates was highly sporadic, and inmates took advantage of that fact.

The medical Department at "Lompoc" left a lot to be desired, as it was nearly impossible to receive any adequate medical care when you were sick.

They tended to believe that an aspirin and a band aid was a cure all for every kind of ailment, regardless of your symptoms.

Inmates that suffered from mental or psychological problems were left untreated, as they were not given proper medications.

Mental disorders accounted for a number of the murders, and contributed to many of the suicides at "Lompoc".

Because of the number of inmates dying at "Lompoc", the convicts had named it:

## "The Valley Of Death"!

Most of the murders were committed with "shanks", or homemade knives. They were easy to make in the work shop, and sold for $30.00 to $50.00 each.

There were so many hiding places at "Lompoc", you could grab a knife at a moment's notice to use if the need arose.

There was an incident at "Lompoc" that cannot be explained. One of the guards a "Captain", turned as white as a sheet one night.

He swears that he saw the "spirit", or "ghost", of a long dead civil war General one night while on duty. No one else there could see the "General", dressed in full military uniform, but this captain had conversations with him.

Many of the other guards there thought that maybe he was losing his mind, but he had never been known to be seeing things that were not there.

During my six years at "Lompoc", there were several attempts by convicts to escape the prison guards.

One was shot dead, and fell off of the fence. Another was shot and wounded, and was cuffed and put in "solitary confinement".

Another was cut up so bad by the razor wire at the top of the fence that he almost bled to death before they could get him to a hospital.

There wasn't much of a "Christian" community here when I arrived, but I tried very hard to correct that.

I started organizing prayer groups, both in English and Spanish, and started Bible study groups too.

There were a lot of men there that were hungry for the "Lord," and I tried to meet their needs as best as I could.

One of the main problems there, though, was the availability of drugs, which were marijuana, heroin and cocaine.

These drugs contribute to most of the death that is prevalent here at "Lompoc".

My fervent prayer, is that the Federal Government will change the administration at "Lompoc", clean it up, replace the guards with professionals that do their jobs correctly, and bring proper medical and psychological help to the inmates housed there.

More "Chapel Services" would help tremendous, along with free Bibles for the inmates that request them.

Amen!

# CHAPTER 17

## "Reaching Out"
### 2003-2006

Farington, New Jersey

When I arrived at "Farington Federal Correctional Institution" in 2003, I was totally amazed by the nice setting of the institution.

They had really good food in the "chow-hall" and you always received good portions of everything, including the desserts, which is my favorite past of each meal, as I have a "sweet tooth".

When I went to the "canteen" for the first time to get some things that I needed, I was pleasantly surprised to find out that the canteens at "Farington" were very well stocked, with plenty of anything you wanted or needed to get, unlike the myriad "Federa Penitentiaries" that I had been incarcerated in before.

The guards at "Farington Correctional Institution" were nice to you, both when you arrived there and went through processing, and during your everyday activities and assignments. This surprised me at first, as I thought that all prison guards were mean and uncaring. But, as I got used to being treated like a human being again, I realized that, at "Farington", they treated you the way that you're supposed to be treated. It was at the "high-security" Federal Penitentiaries that I had been to before, that the prison guards were brutal and violent towards you, supposedly to show you who was in control there

Everyone at "Farington" was very nice to me there.

But most of all, I was very happy and excited to be able to see my family again after many years. My sisters, my cousins, and many of my friends could finally come to visit with me.

Seeing my sister, "Luz", again, after such a long time, almost brought me to my knees. As I hugged her, and kissed her cheeks, and told her how much I loved her and missed her, I broke out in tears and cried like a little baby.

"It's ok, "Juan Pablo", she said as she hugged me back, and comforted me at our first visit there at the visiting room at Farington.

"I'm going to come see you now as much as is possible, hopefully every weekends"! she said to me.

"That would be a dream come true, Luz"; I told her.

"I have missed seeing you and the rest of the family for many years now, 'Luz', and in my heart I almost feel like holding on to you where visiting hours are over, so that you can't go, and leave me alone again in here"; I told her.

"Juan Pablo, when I come back next week, I'll bring your cousin, 'Xiomara', with me, and some others in the family that love you, and want to see you again'; she said.

Tears streamed down my cheeks as I hugged her tightly.

"That would be so wonderful, 'Luz';" I told her, not wanting to let her go as they called out that visiting hours were over.

"I promise I'll be back next week, Juan Pablo. We have so much to talk about, and catch up on."

"Thank you, 'Luz'"; I said as she got up to leave.

As she turned and began walking toward the exit door of the visiting room, she turned around and with large tears in her eyes, ran back to me and gave me a great big hug!

"I love you, 'big brother', and I'll see you in seven days, ok".

"Ok, Luz"; I said, as I smiled broadly at her, and walked her to the door.

As she walked out the door, she turned and smiled brightly, and gave me a little wave, mouthing the words; 'Love You, Juan Pablo'"!

As I left the visiting park, and went to the "security room" for the requisite "contraband search"; I was feeling "happier" than I had felt in a long time.

I missed my family so much, and now the Lord is bringing them back to me again. Thank You, Jesus!

I had always wondered about the way that food is prepared before we eat it, and about all of the different spices that are used in them, plus of the many different techniques used to prepare each dish, like frying, baking, broiling, braising and boiling.

I often wondered how cooks could ever even remember all of the different ways that they have to use to cook our meals, and which techniques were to be used for red meats, pork, veal venison, chicken, turkey, fish and vegetables.

Being in a good institution like Farington motivated me to sign up for their "Culinary Arts" cooking school classes, which they have at Farington.

I took to the classes with "zest, zeal and gusto," paying close attention to everything that was taught in the classes.

I learned of all of the different ways to prepare food, and the more I learned, the more that I wanted to learn.

I wanted to be the best cook that I could become, and I graduated in the top two percent of my class on "Graduation Day"!

I then become the number two cook there, and as soon as the staff and guards found out how good of a cook I was, I become the head cook over staff dining, and prepared all of the food for them that they ate there. That made me feel pretty good!

After I had been there about one year, some of the guys that were members of the "R.O.P.E." reaching out program approached me, and invited me to become a member of the group.

They said that I could be a great contributor to the program, so I gladly accepted their invitation.

As it turned out, their group of fourteen inmates meet at the visiting room at room on every Wednesday.

There, as I found out, we would present our "testimonies" of the crimes that had brought us to prison. This was done in front of children from all walks of life, that were from nine to eighteen years of age, in groups of fifteen to twenty each.

They were accompanied by counselors, and listened attentively as we told them our "life" stories, and of how we ultimately ended up in prison.

We would show them pictures of homemade knives, or "shanks" as they are called behind bars, and photos of other weapons that prisoners use to hurt and kill one another with.

We would also show them photos of prison cells, and the steel beds that we have to sleep on each night, with the sink and toilet that you have to use sometimes in front of your cellmate, explaining that you don't have any privacy in prison.

We would then have an open type discussion, and they would ask us any questions that they had, which were many, usually about our crimes, and about the prison food, etc.

The goal of this program is to reach out to these young people, and to show them how very dangerous "criminal life" is, and to persuade them to not follow our examples in their lives.

Before they left, we would discuss all of the things that happen when you commit a crime, and break the law.

We explain that many people that commit a crime are killed while they are doing it, by the victim of the crime.

Then, their families have to not only "mourn" them, and pay for their funeral, but also suffer "embarrassment" because of the crime that was committed by them.

We also explain that they may end up killing someone while they are committing the crime, which can get them a life sentence, or "death row"!

We tell them that someone usually sees you doing the crime, and turns you in to the police.

We let them know that, after committing a crime, you will always be looking over your shoulder, as you continue to run from the police, never knowing when, or where, they are going to catch you, and arrest you for the crime.

We explain the humiliation of being arrested, and the "strip-search" that you have to go through.

We let them see the large financial burden that they face, or that their family will face, to get them a good lawyer, and the cost of "bail", etc.

We explain that, if convicted of the crime at trial, that they face many years in prisons, away from their family and friends, and loss of their houses, property and job.

We also tell them of how hard it is, once convicted of a felony, to get a good paying job once they get out of prisons, as most employers will not hire someone with a criminal record, or felony conviction.

Before they leave, after about a three hour presentation, we'll have some refreshments with them, such as orange juice and donuts, etc.

For too many young people today feel that a life of crime is "exciting", but it is a one way ticket to prison, and, more often than not, to "death row".

Parents today need to listen to their children, discuss morals with them, teach them right from wrong, show them love, and teach them respect for authority.

Our future, as a nation, is in the hands of our children. We must not fail them.

# CHAPTER 18

## "The Honor Dorm"
### 2006-2009

Levenworth, Kansas

In 2006 I was transferred back to "Levenworth Federal Penitentiary" in Kansas. I was horrified when they told me this, until they explained to me that "Levenworth" was now a "medium security" prison.

Although it's security classification has been lowered to "medium", it will keep its "United States Prison" designation, as it is now designated as an "Historical Site".

They wanted to increase the inmate population with 810 "non"-trouble makers from "Farington Correctional Institution" in New Jersey.

When I arrived back at "Levenworth Federal Penitentiary, I hardly recognized the place, and was surprised at how calm it was now.

Now that it has been lowered to "medium" custody, there is far less trouble there, and almost no killings either.

About a month after I arrived, I got a job in the dental clinic as a dental technician, and was put in charge of the dental lab.

Knowing that I would be leaving here again in three years, I prayed and asked the Lord to lead me to the person He wants me to train as the next dental technician, to take over after I leave.

I waited patiently for his answer, and in March, 2007 I was moved to the "Honor Dorm" to join the "Life Connection Program".

When I arrived at the "Honor Dorm", I was introduced to the community there.

It was there that I met a Christian brother named "Ivan Wiseman".

He had red hair, and blue eyes, and was from the state of "Iowa".

I felt that the Lord had led me to him, and I asked him if he would be interested in the dental program. He then said to me:

"Juan Pablo, you're not going to believe this, but I'm going to be leaving this place in three years, and I have no training many type of trade, to be able to get a job to survive on the streets. I started praying to God, asking Him to find me something, or tell me what to do, as I have nothing when I get to the streets."

The next day, I spoke to my boss at the dental clinic about "Ivan". He is a good Christian man, and he agreed that "Ivan" was a good choice to become the new dental technician at Levenworth.

My boss bought all of the text-books that would be needed, and I started training Ivan for the job, so that he could take over for me after I left.

From the bottom of my heart, I then worked with Ivan every day, and I continued teaching him everything that I knew about dentistry.

I even included the three T's, as I call them, which are "trips, traps and tricks"!

I know that anyone trained in dentistry that is reading this book knows exactly what I am referring to.

Ivan was an excellent student, and he paid close attention to everything that I taught him.

Within a year I was very much amazed at all that Ivan had learned from me.

As it ended up, Ivan had become even a better technician than I am.

I knew that Ivan would do a wonderful job as the new dental technician, and that, when I was transferred from Levenworth, the dental clinic and lab. would be left in very competent hands.

In March 2007, when I joined the "Life Connection Program", I found that it is divided into three phases:

Phase one is:    "Family and Community".
Phase two is:    "Personal Faith" and "Faith in Community".
Phase three is:  "Correct Thinking", alcoholism and Drug addiction and Victim Awareness

In my last semester, and just before I graduated, they brought a group of crime victims into the prison from the free-world, both men and women.

We spent seven days with them, as every day for a week they returned to the prison, and they brought pictures of their loved ones who had been victims of crimes.

They let us know of the pain that they had felt, and the anguish that they had went through, and also of the devastating effects of that experience.

They shared with us how that "crime-event" had changed their lives forever, and how they had lived in fear.

Many of them had spent a lot of money on counseling for their fears and feelings, and on prescribed drugs for their depression and anxiety.

At the end of the week that they had spent with us, they had an "open-microphone" session, where we could ask them questions, or say anything to them.

I want you to keep in mind that I have been trained as a "public-speaker", and I have addressed thousands of people in large groups at various functions.

But, at the end of this week spent with victims of crimes, I found myself paralyzed by the suffering and pain that the victims had went through.

I had never realized that crime could inflict such horrible damage and suffering on people.

When it was my turn to ask questions of these people, I just stood there at the microphone, and couldn't say anything to them.

All I could do was cry, staying quiet for the first time in the seven days they had been there.

I felt so ashamed at that moment, and thought back into my past, and the memories come flooding back to me of my criminal behavior, and the many things that I had done to break the law.

If I could have been granted one wish at that moment, it would have been to go back in time to Medellin, Colombia; to when I was a child, so that I could not steal the coins from my mother's employer's coin box, and stop my life of crime before it ever got started.

The rest of the students in the class were astonished that I had broke down and cried, and could not address the victim's group.

They said: "Juan Pablo, what's wrong? Are you ok"?

"I don't know"! I told them.

But, I knew what it was.

Emotionally, I was overwhelmed at the realization of all of the pain and damage that I had caused in the past by my criminal behavior.

I was so overcome with shame that I couldn't bring myself to speak, and I broke down in front of everyone.

Later, after the victim's group had left, others in the group talked to me.

"Juan Pablo, this is not you"!

"What is going on with you"?

I looked at them for a moment, then tried to explain.

"I felt ashamed, as my past is catching up to me emotionally, and I've realized that my criminal actions hurt people more than I ever knew it could.

It was called "getting real with yourself", and it literally brought me to my knees that day.

Several days later we graduated from the "Life Connection Program", and received our Diplomas.

Not long after that I received a letter from "Senator Brownback" of Kansas, commending me for participating in the "Life Connection Program", and thanking me for my testimony and contribution.

It made me feel so proud to do good things, and receiving a letter from "Senator Brownback" was quite an "honor"!

Soon I would be leaving here, and I would never forget seeing the victim's group, and would always remember the lessons that they have taught me about the pain that crime can cause people.

# CHAPTER 19

# "Florida Bound"
## JUNE 2009-PRESENT

In my heart, mind and soul, I was ready to go home, and my family was waiting for me in New York. I missed them so very badly, and longed to be with them again after twenty five years in Federal Penitentiaries.

But, my dreams of a "Happy homecoming" were shattered by the arrival of two people from the State of Florida, who had come to escort me back to Miami.

On May 29, 2009, at about six in the morning, I was told to pack my property. I was picked up by one man and one woman, and taken to the Kansas City Airport in a caravan of Chevy Suburban S.U.V.'s, with a police escort both in front, and behind us. They weren't playing any games as far as security was concerned.

We boarded the plane before anyone else, and took our seats up in front.

As we took off from the Kansas City airport, I looked out the window and watched as the terrain got smaller and smaller, until we finally ascended up through the clouds at over 35,000 feet.

As we attained cruising altitude and the plane leveled off and throttled back, I leaned my head against the window. Then as I thought of my sister "Luz", my cousin "Xiomara".

My wife "Stella", and the rest of my family that had been waiting for my release, I softly broke down and cried. I had wanted so badly to go home to them.

After landing in Miami, Florida; we were escorted off of the plane before anyone else, and again I was driven in a caravan of "S.U.V.'s" with a police escort until we reached the "Dade County Jail", where I would wait to be taken to a Floridan prison.

Five days later, on June 3, 2009; I was taken from the jail after breakfast, and put on a prison bus, which took me, and several dozen other men, to a place called "South Florida Reception Center", which was about thirty five miles away from the jail.

When we arrived there, we carried our bags of property into the building, and they removed our leg shackles from around our ankles.

I was very glad when they removed them, as mine had been put on much too tight, and my ankles were swollen, and very sore where the blood circulation had stopped, and the shackle had broken the skin and bruised my ankle.

We were then told to strip naked, and stand next to each other. All of the new arrivals, about fifty of us, removed our clothes.

Several prison guards yelled at us, and told us not to move a muscle, to not even twitch.

There were five officers there, four Cubans and one "African-American". They said that if you even scratch your nose they were going to beat the "daylights" out of you.

They then started kicking our property all across the floor. When a couple of the inmates said something about it, they were taken to a back room and worked over. When they returned they were bloody and bruised, and one had a black eye while another had a split lip.

They then stared at all of us, and said: "Anybody else have something to say?"

When nobody spoke up, a "Sergeant" stated:

"Well, it looks like we have another group of spineless pansies to process through"!

One of the guys that was beaten by the guards was next to me, and he had been beaten so badly that he urinated all over my legal work that was on the floor in between us. That kind of put a frown on my face

After we went through the barber shop, where they cut off all of our hair with bare clippers, we were processed through medical and classification, where I was assigned to "H-UNIT".

In "H-UNIT" we were assigned temporary cells, as "South Florida Reception Center" is a processing facility, where new inmates coming into the Florida State Prison System are classified and sent to their permanent camps. You are there anywhere from three to five weeks, depending on your medical or psychological needs, and your security status. I knew that I would be sent to a "closed custody" facility, since I have a "life" sentence to do in Florida.

The cells in "H-UNIT" are filthy, and the toilets are rusty, and clogged up most of the time. the paint is peeling off of everything, from the walls, stairs, rails, floor, and the ceiling too. They haven't performed any real maintenance there in years.

Thirteen days later, on June 16, 2009 I was put into a small bus with about thirty five other men. The bus was called a "Bluebird" Special.

We found out that the bus had no "air conditioning" or proper ventilation, and the temperature quickly reached about 110°F. inside the bus. There was no way for us to cool off.

All we had was a small container of warm water sitting in the back of the bus, and no cups to put the water in to drink.

Right next to the water container is a "stand-up" urinal, and there is no toilet in the bus at all. Since it is a long drive from the "Reception Center" to the institutions we stop at, some of the inmates are forced to use the "urinal" as a toilet, and it was already filled with "human" waste when we boarded the bus.

It stunk very badly in the bus because of this. The flies were thick, and buzzing all around us. We were all sweating profusely, and we had no way to cool-off at all.

The stench became unbearable, and then were several men that got sick and threw up all over the floor of the bus, making the stench even worse.

Added to that was used toilet paper that littered the floor, and the stench of human sweat and body odor and rotten sandwiches and smelly feet. It was very nauseating.

After a fourteen hour trip, we arrived at "Colombia Correctional Institution", which is the "Northern Florida Reception Center" now.

When they opened the door at the back of the "Bluebird" bus, the blast of outside air that washed over us felt cool and fresh, even though it was 100°F. outside. It had to have been 110-115°F. inside the bus.

We all, one by one got off of the bus with our property, and I was very much looking forward to a hot shower.

But, we were made to wait in a hot building while the camp had a count to make sure no one had escaped.

After the count cleared we went through medical processing, which took another one and a half hours.

Finally, we were ordered to go to the dining hall to eat. They told us we were having chicken, but when we received our trays, it looked like they were feeding us "pigeons", because they were so small.

After we finished eating, we were assigned to "D-Dorm", which was air conditioned. It was like a "Godsend" to us, as we were totally exhausted from the long trip on the bus, and we all needed to bathe very badly!

I finally was able to take a hot shower, which I thoroughly enjoyed. After making my bank and laying down after another count, I slept like a little baby. I was asleep as soon as my head hit the pillow.

At three the next morning, they woke everyone up, and we had a quick breakfast before getting back on the "Bluebird Special", that now would be dropping off inmates to different prison camps in the Florida panhandle, which is what they call "Northwestern Florida" here.

I had asked one of the prison guards on the bus, that was riding "shotgun", where I would be going to. He told me that I had been assigned to a prison camp called "Calhoun Correctional Institution" which is located in "Blountstown", Florida.

I had never heard of it, so I asked around to see if anyone had been there before. The man sitting next to me said that he had been there before, and began telling me what the camp was like.

His name was "Meatball"! It was his nickname that he went by because he "loved" (spaghetti) and meatballs with a passion! He was a "chain-smoker", lighting up one after the other. I don't smoke, but I put up with it while he told me about "Calhoun".

He began by telling me that they had really nice, "amazingly clean" dormitories there that were air-conditioned and comfortable. He said that the whole camp was "beautiful", with nice landscaping and flowers blooming everywhere you looked. He said that the nurses were pretty, and the medical care was "top shelf"!

He excitedly told me how great the food was in the dining hall, as he said they had inmates that were former restaurant "chefs" that worked in the kitchen there.

He said that the fried chicken was "fantastic", the Cheese Burgers were "fat and really juicy", with lots of onions and pickles, and had lots of french-fries to go with them. He said it was a great place to be sent to, especially if you liked good "country cooking"!

He described all of the recreational activities they have there, including handball courts. I could hardly wait to get to "Calhoun", as I love to play "handball"!

After a six and a half-hour drive, we finally arrived at "Calhoun Correctional Institution", just outside of Blountstown, Florida. It is located approximately forty miles "North by North East" of Panama City, Florida.

At about nine-thirty in the morning we pulled inside the gate of "Calhoun" C. I. on June 17, 2009.

We then went through property, medical and classification, and I was assigned to "G-Dorm", UNIT 2, and bank forty-five single.

I arrived at the down at eleven-forty-five that morning, just in time to go to lunch.

Talk about your balloon of expectations and hope being suddenly deflated by the sharp needle of reality!

What I found upon entering "G-Dorm" appalled me. I thought I'd entered a "Russian" prison

The beds, mattresses and pillows were all infested with bed bags and blood spots.

The blankets and sheets were full of holes, like in a "Mexican" prison.

The mattresses had no stuffing in them, and they smelled like urine.

The showers were "filthy", as they don't give you proper cleaning chemicals.

My sheets had holes that were big enough for me to crawl through.

As I looked around the down, I noticed a "forlorn" look on most of the men's faces, like they were living in a "nightmare" that they could not escape from.

Most of them were wearing clothes with holes in them, and had shoes that were quite literally falling off of their feet!

Some of them were very needy, to the point that they had to sell their food trays to get necessities like "hygiene" products, or coffee etc..

When we lined up to go to lunch, I had my expectations dashed very quickly when we reached the "chow hall".

The food is not "food", but is like "dog-food", and the portions on the tray are suited for a small child, not an adult.

Instead of having a "thick and juicy" cheese-burger and French fries, with pickles and onions on it, I had a small, thin "soybean" patty that was burned to a crisp. Instead of french-fries, I had two tablespoons of raw potato salad. Instead of lettuce, I had a couple of leaves of cabbage. They also had no salt or pepper to put on this "dog-food" that they are giving us now. The guys call it "kibbles and bits"!

After lunch, which I almost choked on while eating, I opened up a small package of potato chips, which made a "crinkly" sound as I ripped it open. As I started to eat the potato chips, I noticed that it had gotten very quiet in the dorm.

I looked around me, and noticed that most of the guys in the dorm were watching me eat the potato chips, and their mouths were watering as they swallowed repeatedly, longing for something more to eat as they are all still hungry after eating the child portions on their trays.

I felt bad then, and was embarrassed to finish eating the chips. I gave them to an older man sitting on the bank next to mine.

At twelve forty-five that afternoon, I heard them call out that it was time to go to the recreation yard. I looked forward to playing some "hand-ball", and wanted to get some exercise.

My heart fell into my shoes as I walked down the long wide sidewalk to the recreation area. As I looked around the area, I could not see anything that resembled a "hand-ball" court.

I asked another man that was doing pushups where the court was. He said:

"Handball Court"? "What hand-ball court"?

"You mean they don't have one?" I asked.

"Nope, they've never had one here"! He stated.

"What about a weight area. Don't they have a weight training area"?

"No, they took the weights from us about two years ago".

"What do they have here"? I asked him.

"Push-ups, sit-ups, crunches, pull-ups, and basket-ball, and softball in the "Springtime". He replied.

I felt dejected as I walked around the track, which is a dirt path that circles the recreation yard. I had been lied to, and made a fool of by the guy named "Meatball" that I had met that day on the "Bluebird" prison bus.

There was little at this camp as far as "recreation" was concerned, and the "dog-food" in the "chow-hall" isn't even considered worth consuming by human beings! I felt miserable as I slowly trudged my way back to the dorm when the whistle blew, ending recreation time, which lasted about forty-five minutes.

I introduced myself to the "Christian" community there in "G-Dorm", and in doing so I met a man named "Alex Samurai".

As I talked with him, and exercised with him on the recreation yard, and attended chapel services with him, I found him to be a highly intelligent man.

He began showing me around the camp, and explained how the Florida Prison System worked.

He told me of the gangs, and of the people that I shouldn't associate with, that would help me to stay away from trouble here.

In talking about his life, "Al" explained that he had went to "Russia" in 1981 for 18 months of military training from his homeland of "Portugal".

After his military training in Russia was completed, he want to "Brazil", and become a Military Intelligence Officer from 1983-1984.

In 1984 he "defected" to the United States, and was "debriefed" by both the "C.I.A". and the "F.B.I"., which also polygraphed him.

After being evaluated by the "C.I.A". and "F.B.I.", he was granted "refugee" status.

In 1985, he moved to "Canada", where he stayed till 1987.

In 1987 he moved to "France", where he joined the "French Foreign Legion". There, he met his wife.

In 1988 he left the "French Foreign Legion" and moved back to "Canada".

Finally, in 1989 he returned to the "United States", where he was again "debriefed" by the C.I.A.

He has lived in the "United States" since then, having moved to Florida.

"Al Samurai" is an expert in several "Martial Arts", which include Brazilian "JU-JITSU", and also the Japanese "Martial Art" of "Kiyo-Ko-Shinki".

He has explained to me that he had called himself a "Christian" for most of his life, but that it wasn't until the year 2001 that he was "Saved By The Grace Of God" and truly. "Born-again" as one of God's children.

Now, he not only "talks the talk" as a Christian, but he actually "walks the walk" as well!

He has become a very close friend to me here, as well as a fine "Christian brother".

I have found that he is "well-connected" as to government agencies, who sometimes ask for his help in translating several difficult languages.

He speaks five different languages, which include English, Russian, French, Portuguese, and Arabic, which include the Farsi and Pashtu dialects.

He also knows how to were money from one place to another that is totally "untraceable".

As I started walking around the recreation yard with "Al", and meeting others on the compound, he introduced me to a good friend of his that everyone calls "Radio-Shock".

His actual name is "Enrique Cardenas", and he is called "Radio-Shock" because he is an electronics "whiz" that can repair anything electronic on the compound, including televisions, radios, headphones etc.

He can also repair combination locks, and fix glasses when someone breaks theirs.

I was very glad to meet "Enrique", as I began to send him radios, headphones and glasses to fix for people that I was helping out, that could not afford to get them fixed themselves.

As time passed, and I got to know Enrique Cardenas even better, I found out that he was so much "more" than a great "electronics" man. He is also an expect automotive technician, and highly knowledgeable on aviation.

He turned out to be a pretty amazing guy, as not only can he repair electronics, he is also well educated, with an extremely high "I. Q." score. He has a "phenomenal" memory also.

As Enrique and I talked more with each other, and shared our life stories and Christian testimonies with each other Enrique Cardenas inspired me to have this book written by my sister "Luz" and cousin "Xiomara" in New Jersey.

He said that I had what he described as an extraordinary life story, and that people need to hear my story and "testimony", as it could deter young people from making the mistakes that I've made, that started a life of crime.

My friend, "Enrique", has been invaluable to me in the past twenty-two months, both as an inspiration to share my story with the world, and as a good "Christian" brother with a heart of gold. Like many other men and women in our nation's prisons, he has been abandoned by his family while in prison, and has no one on the outside who cares about him anymore, or who will help him.

His crime was in shooting and killing a man named "Christopher Morris" in Pompano Beach, Florida in 1990, that had taken his father's gun, and was going to kill his estranged wife and step-daughter for their life insurance money. I believe he had a trial that was held in a "kangaroo" court, and I pray that someday he can obtain an adequate lawyer that can straighten out the mess he found himself in when in "Pompano Beach". He is a good "Christian" man, and I believe he deserves a second chance. He has been in prison now for over 21 on a 25 "mandatory", and we'll be eligible for parole in January 2015. I pray that he is released then.

My life now in Calhoun Correctional Institution is in Ministering to inmates here in both English and Spanish Bible Studies that I conduct on the recreation yard, and in helping those in need that I can help.

This ministry is made possible by my sister "Luz", and my cousin "Xiomara", in New Jersey, and my wife "Stella".

They make phone calls to different countries to tell an inmate's family and friends that he is alright, and to give them information on how to contact the inmate.

Here in Calhoun Correctional Institution I wait for the Lord to fulfill His third promise to me, of being released, and sharing my testimony with the world.

# E P I L O G U E

The purpose of writing this book is not to "glamorize" the criminal life, but to help people to make the right choices in life before it is too late to do so.

I want to make people aware of the danger, violence, destruction and pair and ultimate death in leading a life of crime.

Hollywood portrays criminals as romantic and sexy and exciting, but that is only a filmed "illusion"!

I beg you from the bottom of my heart to ask "God" for strength for you to change if you are already involved in the criminal life, even at a minor role, and not to get into a life of crime if you haven't yet.

I don't want you to go through all of the horrors that I've went through, and find yourself tied up in chains and locked up like I am now.

I hope and pray that my story gets through to you before it is too late, and that my "Lord" will open your eyes, and your heart and stop you before you are pulled into the fires of Hell by this "Fatal Illusion".

"Amen"!

Juan Pablo Castillo
April, 2011

# WHERE ARE THEY NOW?

1982 "Adrian"

In 1982 "Adrian" stole $ 11,000,000.00 dollars from another gang that he had dealings with, and was killed by them when they found out it was him.

They had called him, and told him that they had another deal for him. He was given a location to meet them at.

When he arrived and discussed the deal with them, he was "machine-gunned" and shot 18 times. He was in his mid 40's when killed.

1984 "Jonathan"

Jonathan betrayed "Marcos", and told the "Medellin Cartel" that Marcos was no good.

Marcos waited for Jonathan to come out of his house one morning, and "machine-gunned" him to death with 33 bullets!

Jonathan died at the age of 42 years old.

1985 "Swede"

Swede was in "Bogota", the capital of Colombia. He was "machine-gunned" to death coming out of a bank that he had just robbed, and fell dead in the bank's doorway, with a bullet in his head, and 29 other bullets in his body from the police.

There was no need for him to rob the bank, or be killed, as he was already a "multi-millionaire" from previous robberies, and the cocaine drug trade. He was in his mid 50's when killed by the authorities.

### 1987 "Marcos"

Marcos was found in an open field in "Medellin", Colombia, with his hands full of grass. He had been pulled by his ankles backwards", and had clawed at the ground to try to save himself from being killed.

He had been shot in each "kneecap", and in each shoulder, and his phallus had been cut off and stuffed into his mouth. He was dead at 55 years of age.

### 1988 "El-Pivā"

"El-Pivā" retired, gathered up all of his money and quietly disappeared to start a business somewhere. At the age of 32 yrs. old.

### 1990 "Alphonso"

Alphonso also made a decision to retire. He had millions put away, and moved to "Australia". He was never heard from again. He disappeared at 57 years of age.

### Present Day-2011 "Juan Pablo Castillo"

Jailed in 1984, baptized and "saved" by the Grace of God in 1987! Served 25 years in Federal Penitentiaries.

Presently serving a "life" sentence in Florida at "Calhoun Correctional Institution" in Blountstown, Florida.

1995 "Hugo"

Had evaded prosecution in 1984 by fleeing to "Costa-Rica".

Tried to leave "Costa-Rica" in 1995 using his own real name and "passport \ Visa", and was arrested on an "International Warrant" from "Interpol" for 1ST. Degree Murder and Kidnapping.

He received 40 years in Federal Prison in the "United States".

"Present Status" – Unknown!

*I dedicate this book to my mother and to my siblings.*

*I would like to thank Norma Fermaint and Claudia Duque for making the publication of this book possible.*